MINISTRY OF HOME SECURITY

AIR RAIDS
What You must know
What You must do

The Naval & Military Press Ltd

Published by

The Naval & Military Press Ltd

Unit 5 Riverside, Brambleside
Bellbrook Industrial Estate
Uckfield, East Sussex
TN22 1QQ England

Tel: +44 (0)1825 749494

www.naval-military-press.com
www.nmarchive.com

CONTENTS

2

3

LIST OF ILLUSTRATIONS

FOREWORD

BY

SIR JOHN ANDERSON, G.C.B., G.C.S.I., G.C.I.E., M.P.

Minister of Home Security.

This book is written to help you and your family and your friends.

There has been built up in the last few years a vast organisation for Civil Defence; and, thanks to the devotion of a great army of volunteers, the services which it comprises have been welded into a highly efficient force. This organisation is briefly described in the first chapter, which has been included in this book for two reasons; first, because I may, in the near future, have to call on many of you to give some part of your time to one or other of these services, and secondly, because you may need the help of the services and should therefore understand something about them.

But the Civil Defence services alone cannot protect you from the consequences of air raids. Your own protection and the protection of your family must, in large measure, depend on your taking certain necessary precautions. You can yourself do much to minimise risk to yourself and to those dependent on you.

A great deal of information has been collected as a result of experience gained in actual air raids, and from this and from research and experiment the basic principles on which the protection of life and limb and property depends have been worked out and are set down here for your guidance. They are simple to understand and easy to carry out; and if you will act on them you will be able to face the dangers of air raids with the sure conviction that you have done all in your power for the safety of those depending on you, and with the calmness and assurance that come from a knowledge of the way in which these dangers can be met. In this way you will be helping not only yourself, but the Nation, for it is through the strengthening of your powers of resistance that the people of this country will be enabled to defeat every attempt the enemy may make to weaken its morale and paralyse its war effort.

In this war every man and woman is in the front line. A soldier at the front who neglects the proper protection of his trench does more than endanger his own life; he weakens a portion of his country's defences and betrays the trust which has been placed in him. You, too, will have betrayed your trust if you neglect to take the steps which it is your responsibility to take for the protection of yourself and your family.

This is a contribution to the winning of final victory which you personally can make and which no one else can make for you. I am confident that you will make it.

Ministry of Home Security.

June, 1940.

CHAPTER 1

THE CIVIL DEFENCE SERVICES.

Introductory.

The object of enemy air raids is to dislocate the war effort of the nation. The attainment of this object may be sought by deliberate attacks on targets of military significance, a term having a wide application in these days, or by unrestricted and indiscriminate bombing of the civil population. The primary responsibility for resisting the enemy's efforts lies with the active defence services. But it is essential to have available a nation-wide organisation, the purpose of which is to minimise the effects of air raids by such aircraft as succeed in penetrating the active defences. Such an organisation, known as Civil Defence, has been built up and forms what might now be referred to as the Fourth Defence Service. The operation of this service is the responsibility of local authorities in the United Kingdom, working under the general direction of the Ministry of Home Security.

The tactics of bombing from the air vary from mass raids by large numbers of bombers to attacks by small numbers of aircraft or even by single machines. Attacks may be launched in single raids with long intervals between each raid, or in successive raids following closely upon each other both by day and by night, and maintained over an extended period.

Whatever form aerial attack takes, damage of some kind is inevitable, and the lives of many civilians will be endangered, unless certain essential elementary knowledge is previously gained, and a number of simple precautions observed.

The most effective weapon for causing major damage from the air is probably the high explosive bomb. Its destructive effects are immediate, and it is a difficult weapon against which to provide complete protection except at a very high cost. To cause numerous major fires simultaneously over a wide area may also be an enemy objective, and this may be done by means of incendiary bombs, particularly those of the lighter type, thousands of which could be dropped at one time upon a densely built-up area. Machine-gun fire also may be directed from low-flying aircraft upon persons exposed to the raiders. The possibility of poison gas being used, though it is forbidden by the Geneva Gas Protocol of 1925, cannot be overlooked, and such attacks might be made either by bomb or spray or both.

All these weapons of air attack may be used by themselves or in effective combinations devised to cause the greatest dislocation of the war effort of the nation, and to threaten the morale of the people.

The Organisation of Civil Defence.

There is much that citizens can do, and which no one can do for them, to help themselves, their families, and the nation, but it has been necessary to set up in addition the great organisation of Civil Defence, built principally on unpaid voluntary service, for the discharge of the many skilled duties described below. Everyone should understand this organisation, both so that he may

7

be able to help so far as he is able, and so that he may not fail to take advantage, in case of need, of the services which have been set up.

The Warning System.

A means by which warning of an approaching raid can be given to the general public is of first importance, and this is provided by a national system. Warning messages are sent out to the districts where air attack may materialise, and in those districts only is the "Action Warning" sounded by sirens. The signal is a "warbling" note given on a variable-pitch siren, or a succession of 5-second blasts sounded on a fixed-pitch hooter followed by intervals of 3 seconds. The warning is then taken up locally by sharp blasts on police and wardens' whistles.

When the raid has passed or is no longer expected, this is announced by a continuous blast, known as the "Raiders Passed" signal. All siren signals are sounded for a period of two minutes.

If the presence of gas is suspected, warning of it is given locally by wardens' hand-rattles; and when the area is known to be safe again, this warning is cancelled by the ringing of wardens' handbells. Handbells may also be sounded to inform the public when it is again safe to emerge from shelter, if sirens are put out of action as the result of a raid.

Air-Raid Wardens.

There will be a great need in time of air raids for persons of courage and personality, with a sound knowledge of the locality, to advise and help their neighbours, and generally to serve as a link between the public and the authorities. To provide for this, the Air Raid Wardens' Service has been organised, based on a large number of local Posts.

Wardens have important duties to carry out, including assessing air-raid damage, reporting it concisely and correctly, guiding and assisting the A.R.P. services sent to deal with it, and giving general assistance and guidance to members of the public. Their functions are in some respects allied to those of the police, with whom they will need to co-operate closely; and, though they are not part of the police or special constabulary, the wardens' service is generally placed by the local authority under the executive control of the Chief Constable.

It is important that everyone should know the names and addresses of the nearest Wardens and the position of the Warden's reporting post, since it may be necessary as a result of air-raid damage to make immediate contact with a Warden, or to arrange for the making of an urgent report.

Auxiliary Fire Service.

It is important that fires should be tackled as soon as they are started, as they are very much more easily put out at this stage than later. Incendiary bombs may cause fires in such large numbers in a comparatively restricted area that the normal resources of the Fire Brigade will be inadequate. An Auxiliary Fire Service has therefore been formed and trained to reinforce the regular fire brigades. The fire brigade equipment has also been increased by the provision, on loan to the local authorities, of large numbers of pumping units, mainly trailer pumps, drawn by cars, taxis, vans or lorries, but including also self-propelled units where required. Emergency fire floats have also been added to the fire brigade equipment in a number of areas.

First-Aid Parties.

There may be injured who must be given attention where they lie; some will require removal for further treatment. For this work there are First Aid (or Stretcher) Parties, each consisting of four men with a driver and transport for themselves and vehicles for the injured provided by the Ambulance Service.

First-Aid Posts and Hospitals.

There must be places where the lightly and seriously injured can be treated, and this is done at First-Aid Posts and Hospitals. First-Aid Posts are normally in buildings adapted and equipped for this work. They are supplemented by Mobile Units, consisting of vehicles in which the appropriate equipment and staff are conveyed to scenes of damage in order that temporary First-Aid Posts may be established nearby.

In rural districts First-Aid Points are established, and consist of a first-aid box placed in some central building where attention to the injured can be given.

The position of First-Aid Posts and Points should be known to all who live in the vicinity, for it may be necessary for slightly wounded persons to go there on foot, or for uninjured persons to convey a neighbour, for the purpose of obtaining first aid.

Rescue Parties.

Those who have been trapped in shelters or under buildings must be released. This work requires experience and care, since debris unskilfully moved might release other parts of the structure, and so cause it to crash upon both rescuers and those to be rescued.

This work is done by Rescue Parties, who will also undertake the temporary shoring up or the demolition of partly collapsed buildings where these are a source of immediate danger and the work is within their scope. As it is probable that many of the trapped will be injured, at least four members of each Rescue Party are also trained and equipped to render first aid.

For certain parts of rescue party work, for example, the removal by manhandling of piled-up debris, Rescue Parties may ask for the assistance of able-bodied members of the public who are available nearby.

Demolition and Repair Parties.

After an air raid extensive demolition work may have to be done, streets cleared of wreckage, craters filled in, and fractured gas, water, and electricity mains and sewers may need repair. Such work may have to be carried out urgently in order to remove danger, or for the purpose of restoring essential services. Work of this kind will be undertaken by parties obtained from local authorities' staffs or the staffs of public utilities as required, or from contractors, according to the particular work to be undertaken.

In clearing wreckage, demolition and repair parties may, like Rescue Parties, utilise the services of members of the public who are willing to help.

Gas Identification Service.

If poison gas is used, wardens will immediately report the fact. They will also warn the public. There may arise problems in connection with gas warfare, however, which require the services of experts, and to provide for this a local Gas Identification Service, consisting of specially trained chemists and assistants, has been formed and equipped with apparatus suitable for their specialised duties.

Decontamination Squads.

Areas where persistent gas has fallen are said to be contaminated, and are dangerous until the gas has been neutralised or removed. The work of decontamination is related generally to that of the Street Cleansing Services, and special Decontamination Squads, consisting of a foreman and five men with the addition of a driver, have been recruited, principally from these services, for the work.

Treatment of Unexploded Bombs and Wrecked Aircraft.

Bombs from enemy aircraft or shells from our own anti-aircraft guns may fall without exploding; these are a potential source of danger, and their presence and exact position should be immediately reported to a Warden or the Police. They will then be removed or destroyed by parties specially trained in this work, and in the meantime they should not be touched.

Similarly, a crashed enemy aircraft is also dangerous. If it catches fire, the petrol, ammunition, and any bombs still remaining in their racks may explode. If the aircraft is not on fire, there still remains a possible danger of explosion.

It will be the duty of Wardens and the Police to keep the public away from unexploded bombs, shells, and crashed enemy aircraft, and to arrange, as necessary, that nearby buildings are vacated until the area has been made safe by the appropriate means.

Report and Control Centres.

For the operation and control of all A.R.P. services, there must be local headquarters to receive damage reports and to issue instructions for the despatch of the necessary parties to scenes of damage. For this purpose Report and Control Centres have been established. These are manned by telephonists, messengers, clerks, and representatives of the various A.R.P. services, who are co-ordinated by an Officer-in-Charge.

A Report and Control Centre may be combined, or there may be one or more Report Centres linked to the Control Centre, which is the nerve-centre of the local organisation and the headquarters from which local operations are directed.

A.R.P. Controllers.

The local A.R.P. services are under the general charge of an A.R.P. Controller, whose duty it is to maintain the smooth and efficient working of the various A.R.P. services of the local organisation and who is supremely responsible for their operations in times of raiding.

CHAPTER 2

SELF-PROTECTION AGAINST HIGH EXPLOSIVE BOMBS, AND BEHAVIOUR DURING A RAID.

High Explosive Bombs and Their Effects

A high explosive bomb consists of a charge of high explosive mixture contained in a steel case fitted with a fuse and exploder.

The destructive effects are twofold : those of blast, i.e. the air pressure and waves created by the explosion, and those of fragmentation, i.e. the breaking up of the steel case of the bomb into jagged pieces or splinters.

Splinters.

The average size of these splinters is about 1 in. across, and they are projected in large numbers in every direction at about twice the speed of a rifle bullet. On striking a hard surface they may be arrested or, if deflected in their path, may cause damage from an unexpected direction.

The effective range of splinters can be considerable, and unless sufficient resistance is encountered in their path, they may inflict fatal injury at points as far distant as half a mile from the fall of the bomb.

Blast.

Blast is more freakish in the havoc it brings and a detailed treatment of the subject would involve a technical description of scientific phenomena. It is sufficient to say here that on the bursting of a bomb there is a violent outward movement of air in the immediate vicinity of the explosion, followed instantly by a great inrush of air causing a momentary suction. A shock-wave is created and travels at a velocity, in the first instant, greater than that of sound; but it quickly becomes weaker as it goes. If the explosion takes place after penetration of the ground surface, corresponding waves are also set up in the earth.

In the immediate vicinity of the bomb, shock-waves may completely destroy buildings or may partially destroy them by causing the collapse of wall panels, roofs, doors, and windows. These are the " near effects," caused by pressure or suction.

Further away, only structures of light construction, such as prominent balconies, and roof tiles and slates, plaster from ceilings, and window glass are likely to be affected. These are the " distant effects," caused by violent shaking.

It can never be predicted, especially in the case of doors and windows subjected to the near effects of blast, whether they will be blown violently inwards or sucked outwards. It can, however, be said that the glass of unprotected windows will almost certainly be shattered, and that the flying jagged pieces will be a source of the utmost danger.

Window glass subjected to distant effects of blast may also be shattered, but with considerably less violence, the fracture being caused by the resonance set up in the panes by the shock wave. If windows are left wide open they are less likely to be broken. It is advisable, however, to close them if a gas warning is given, and bombing is not in progress at the time.

Far greater areas are exposed to the distant effects of bombs than to the near effects, and consequently the chance of a house being subjected to distant effects is far greater than that of its suffering nearer effects.

Types of H.E. Bombs.

There are certain types of H.E. bombs, such as anti-personnel and armour-piercing bombs, designed for attack on specific objectives, but the most commonly used are the General Purpose types. The latter, as the name implies, are employed for general bombardment purposes and are used, for example, against factories and buildings of ordinary construction.

These bombs may be fitted with fuses to detonate them on impact or after a delay varying within a considerable time range; normally they have fuses giving a delay action of a few tenths of a second in order that the target may be penetrated before detonation, but the delay can be increased to many minutes or even longer periods.

The weights of bombs vary greatly. In determining the size of bomb to be used, account has to be taken of the carrying capacity of the aircraft, the weight of fuel required, and the destructive effect of the different weights of bombs. In the present circumstances, the bombs most generally in service are of about 100 lb., 250 lb., and 500 lb.; such bombs are between 4 and 5 feet long; and from 9 to 15 ins. in diameter.

High Bombing Attacks.

Hostile aircraft will be subjected to heavy anti-aircraft fire from our home defence units. Over certain vulnerable parts of the country, barrage balloons, too, will add to the hazards with which they must contend, and at all times there will be the Fighter machines of the R.A.F. launching fierce attacks upon the enemy.

These defences will tend to cause raiding units to keep as far out of range as they can, consistent with the requirements of their plan of bombing. In many cases, therefore, the majority of bombing attacks over this country may be expected to be launched from a considerable height.

There are two points arising from this source which are of special interest to the civilian population.

Firstly, even if it could be assumed that the enemy would confine his attention to military targets, the small measure of accuracy obtainable when bombs are released from a great height leaves a wide margin as regards the possible positions where the bombs might actually fall. Some may fall in the areas at which they are aimed, whilst others would almost certainly fall in residential areas, the suburbs of cities, or even in parks, fields, or rivers. Every citizen, then, must realise that he and his family are among the potential victims of air attack, and that he must take all possible steps to secure protection.

Secondly, bombs released from modern aircraft flying at great heights and speeds must be released well before the target is reached. Anyone who waits till he sees aeroplanes overhead before taking cover is thus running the gravest risk of being injured by the bursting of a bomb dropped before the bomber comes into sight—for in congested areas in particular it is most unlikely that there will be clear view of the sky for many miles in all directions.

Low Flying Attacks and Machine Gunning.

Where there is no balloon barrage, attacks may be made from very low altitudes, or by dive-bombing, and aircraft may skim over the roof-tops spraying unprotected persons in the streets and at windows with machine-gun bullets.

Other Falling Projectiles.

In addition to the dangers resulting from H.E. and machine gun attacks, and from incendiary bomb and gas attacks described in later chapters, there are other falling missiles inseparable from the presence of hostile aircraft over this country. Anti-aircraft shells are designed to explode in the air, and the fragments of metal, including the heavy nose-cap, will descend upon the country below. Expended machine gun bullets resulting from aerial combat will also fall to the ground.

The Importance of Shelter.

These, then, are some of the dangers which air raids will bring. Outside the very small area in which the severest consequences of a direct hit are felt, there is a large area in the case of each bomb explosion in which there are the gravest dangers to life for the unprotected, as has been explained in the foregoing pages, but against which it is perfectly practicable to provide protection simply and cheaply. Every time a bomb explodes in a congested area, for a large number of people in the vicinity it may make the difference between life and death whether or not they have provided themselves with shelter and, on hearing the sirens, have taken refuge in it.

A vital responsibility therefore lies on each householder to ensure that adequate shelter is available for himself and his dependents. In order to assist persons who wish to avail themselves of expert advice as regards the selection of the form of shelter best suited to their own case, certain of the Professional Institutions have arranged, with the approval of the Government, to set up a panel of Engineers, Architects, and Surveyors who are competent to give technical advice to householders. For the sum of 10s. 6d. a member of the panel will inspect the house and give the householder a brief written report as to the best place for a shelter and the best way within his means to provide protection.

A list of consultants on the panel has been furnished to certain local authorities and on application to the authority a householder may obtain a list of consultants from which to choose. If the authority has no such list, application should be made to The Secretary, Central Board, 1-7 Great George Street, Westminster, London, S.W.1, who will provide the name or names of consultants available near the householder who applies.

Provision of a Refuge in the House.

In many cases it will be found that the most convenient means of providing a shelter is to adapt some part of the existing premises for the purpose, and this is something which very often a handy man can do for himself, using largely materials which he can find in his own house or garden.

Full-scale experiments conducted with 500-lb. bombs have shown that, outside a radius of 50 ft. from the point of burst, the average well-built house of normally substantial construction should give its occupants substantial protection against the effect of blast and splinters, as well as against machine-gun bullets and light missiles, subject to certain provisions being made. Windows and doorways should be blocked up or protected in some other way; ceilings must be supported in case of the collapse of the roof or upper storey; where walls are thinner than 13½ ins. of sound brickwork or stonework or the equivalent of this, they must be reinforced by the addition of further material, such as earth in boxes piled beside the wall to a height of at least 6 ft.

Selection of a Refuge.

The considerations may broadly be divided into two parts; those of lateral protection, that is, protection from blast and splinters provided by

13

side walls, and those of overhead protection against light incendiary bombs, fragments of anti-aircraft shells, machine gun bullets, etc., and against the fall of debris, should the upper parts of the building collapse.

Basement and semi-basement rooms offer the best natural protection, since lateral protection is generally wholly or partly provided by their sunken position, and they probably have fewer windows to be blocked or protected than other rooms. As regards overhead protection, there are all the floors and the roof of the building above them to give protection from falling objects, though they may not possess adequate strength to take the load of the building should it collapse. It is desirable to obtain professional guidance as to whether the ceiling is capable of taking the weight of falling debris, and, if not, how best it can be strengthened for the purpose.

Where there is no basement, it will usually be advisable to select a room on the ground floor or one of the lower floors, in order to ensure good overhead protection against falling missiles; wherever possible there should be two floors and a roof above the shelter. Rooms on higher floors are inconvenient to adapt, since it may be necessary to protect the floor from splinters striking up through a window of the room below, and the strengthening of the ceiling also is most difficult and often impossible to arrange.

In the case of rooms at or above ground level, it is necessary to consider the thickness of the walls upon which lateral protection will depend. A shelter should, if possible, be protected by $13\frac{1}{2}$ in. of sound brickwork or stonework on all sides. It is not necessary that the walls of the shelter room itself should everywhere be of this thickness, provided there are other walls within a distance of about 30 ft. which give on all sides a total thickness equivalent to $13\frac{1}{2}$ ins. of solid brick or stone; if in any direction this degree of protection is not afforded by the premises as they stand, additional material should if possible be added. If it is not practicable to provide a thickness of $13\frac{1}{2}$ ins. in all directions, a single 9-in. wall of sound brick or stone will give considerable protection.

Other things being equal, rooms facing soft ground, such as gardens and fields, are more suitable for use as shelters than those looking out on a street or hard paving, since the destructive effects of a bomb bursting in soft soil are not so great as those of one in contact with a hard surface.

Persons living in the upper storeys of houses converted into flats will need to come to some arrangement with the other occupants so that common protection can be secured for all in the manner most suitable to all the circumstances. Those living on the ground floor or in the basement might give up space in an entrance hall or passage, whilst others might provide material and labour for blocking up a window or making other structural adaptations, or it might be possible to adapt quite simply a common staircase for use as a refuge by all.

Protection of Windows and Doors.

After a suitable room has been selected as a refuge, the windows and any outside doors will need to be given special protection. Windows in particular are highly vulnerable to both splinters and blast, and even when situated below ground, and thus protected against splinters, they may still be affected by blast. Moreover, they may be broken by the vibrations set up by distant effects in situations where no splinters can reach them.

Protection against Splinters.

One method of protecting windows against splinters is to remove the window frame and fill in the opening with brickwork of the same thickness as the wall. Another method is to build, outside the window, a wall of brickwork

14

13¼ inches thick, or of earth or sand 30 inches thick, or of ballast or broken bricks 24 inches thick; where materials other than brick are used, they may be contained in boxes, or held between boards or corrugated sheet iron.. Protection can also be improvised by placing boxes tightly packed with books to a thickness of at least 24 inches against the inside of the window.

Protective walls for windows should extend completely across the opening, overlapping it by one foot on each side and at the top also.

A saving can be made in the materials used to provide protection by erecting them on a strong platform or table placed at least one foot below the window to obviate building up the walling from the ground level.

As far as bomb splinters are concerned, protection need not extend above 6 feet from the floor, as persons in the refuge will then be safe from such splinters, though the window will, of course, be vulnerable to blast.

Similar protection can be given to doorways in outside walls, provided the entrances do not have to be used, except possibly under force if other ways of exit become blocked. Where the door is a regular means of entrance and must be kept free, a substantial traverse should be built to a height of at least 6 feet and to a width greater than that of the doorway, and 3 or 4 feet away from it.

Protection against Blast.

Windows and doors which are fully protected against splinters by the foregoing methods will generally be protected against blast. But there will be

A stout book-case, stuffed tightly with old books, protects one window. Or a table can be used with books 2 ft. 6 in. thick piled on it. If the books are loose they should be roped down firmly.

many windows of a house, notably those of rooms other than the one adapted for use as a shelter, which will cause great inconvenience if shattered. No protection can be obtained simply for these against near effects, but some measure of reinforcement can be given to them against distant effects and the risk of small pieces of glass flying about reduced by one of the following means :—

(1) A piece of fabric such as muslin, calico, cotton, or linen sheeting may be pasted all over the glass. A variety of adhesives can be used, such as office paste, gum, size, paperhanger's paste, or ordinary flour paste with an addition of treacle or glycerine in the proportion of one part of treacle or glycerine to twenty parts of the adhesive. Waterglass (sodium silicate) should not be used. The glass should be well coated with the adhesive. Where the loss of light does not matter, a strong cardboard may be pasted over the glass. In order to make the cardboard stick, its natural curvature should be noted and it should be placed with its hollow side, which may also be coated with the adhesive, facing the glass and then be pressed firmly in contact. When there is not enough cardboard available a strong wrapping paper can be used, but it will not be equally effective.

(2) The inner face of the glass may be sprayed or painted with a liquid composition of which special varieties can be bought. These materials mostly have only a limited life, and may have to be renewed after about two or three months.

(3) A transparent film of the kind used for wrapping may be applied to the inner face of the glass. It can be pasted over the whole window, or it can be applied in strips at right-angles. There are several materials of this kind and each requires the proper adhesive. The makers' directions should be followed closely.

(4) Where none of the above recommendations can be followed, materials can be applied in strips, though they do not prevent glass from splintering quite so well as all-over coverings. Surgical plaster or insulating tape are useful and are best pressed on with a warm iron. Strips of wrapping paper are not so satisfactory because they tear more easily. The strips should not be more than 6 inches apart.

In all cases in which glass is retained in the windows of refuge rooms, unless the opening has been wholly blocked, it is essential to arrange protection against the violent scattering of broken glass by one or other of the foregoing methods.

Keeping out wind and rain when windows are broken.

If window panes are shattered, it will be necessary to keep out wind and rain and possibly poison-laden air. For this purpose, a shutter made of wall-boarding, plywood, or other stout material fixed to a light wooden frame, accurately fitting the window opening and having felt or thick cloth tacked around the edges, is recommended. This wall-board shutter should not be secured in position except by the friction of its close fit assisted by the felt around its edges; it will thus not offer resistance to blast, and, if blown away from the window, will fall into the room undamaged and can be easily replaced. It will be found useful to attach the top edge of the shutter to the wall by two lengths of stout rubber about 18 inches long, so that, while it is left free to swing from the window, it will be prevented from flying across the room.

16

Alternatively, shutters made of wood 2 inches thick throughout may be fixed on the outside of the window. These wooden shutters must be firmly clamped to the wall, for instance, by iron bars fixed across them with the ends securely fastened to the wall. While such shutters will not prevent the glass from being broken by blast, they will themselves normally withstand the effects of blast, and, if fitted with the necessary gaskets, will also keep out poison-laden air.

Provision of a Shelter Outside the House.

In some cases it may be decided to provide a shelter of special construction outside the house. Such a shelter may take one of several forms and may be situated in the garden, if there is one, or nearby, wherever accommodation permits.

Arrangements may be made with neighbours for two or more householders to share the expenditure of a commercially built structure situated conveniently to all.

The entrance of such shelter must always be protected from splinters either by means of a substantial traverse or by proximity to a substantial building or wall. The shelter should be sited not nearer to any building than half the height of that building. Where this cannot be achieved, the roof of the shelter must be made strong enough to resist the fall of debris.

Generally it is found that the proper siting and erection of outside shelters are matters for the building and contracting profession. For that reason, only brief notes are given in the pages which follow on the various types of outside shelters, sufficient to indicate the kind of problems to be tackled. Those wishing to provide for themselves specially made shelters are recommended to make contact direct with the profession or to approach the local Council for guidance, whichever is more appropriate.

Types of Shelters independent of Buildings.

Shelters independent of buildings may take the form of covered trenches or they may be special constructions, lined for example with steel or concrete.

Trenches.

Being constructed wholly or partly below ground, trenches afford excellent lateral protection, but they must be given overhead cover against light falling missiles. This requires a head cover of 5 inches of concrete or 18 to 24 inches of earth. More earth should not be used, because, in the event of collapse, the occupants of the shelter might be so deeply buried as to be unable to extricate themselves.

Trenches should provide not less than 6 feet of head room and should be fitted with seats. They must be lined with strong materials to prevent the walls from collapsing, and should be provided with a form of floor covering, such as duckboards or shingle.

Arrangements must be made to drain away any water which may seep into the trench.

Government Steel Shelters (" Anderson Shelters ").

Corrugated steel shelters made in sections to accommodate four or more persons made to Government specification have been distributed in large numbers in the more vulnerable areas.

The sections of these shelters fit together in the form of an arch designed to carry the necessary covering of earth for overhead protection against falling

A Completed Anderson Shelter.

splinters and debris. Where possible, they should be sunk about 3 feet into the ground, and should invariably be covered with earth to a minimum depth of 15 ins. over the arch. These shelters do not provide the required protection unless covered by at least this thickness of earth. The shelter should be sited from 6 to 15 feet away from a building in such a position that the building protects the entrance from splinters.

Surface Shelters.

These are built entirely above the ground; they may be constructed of 15 inches of concrete, 12 inches of reinforced concrete, or 13½ inches of brickwork. Overhead cover must be provided against the fall of light missiles, and for this purpose reinforced concrete 5 inches thick may be used.

General Notes on Shelters.

Before a refuge or shelter can be considered to be completed and equipped, there are certain points to which attention must be directed. It is important that these matters be attended to immediately the accommodation is available and not left until just before or during an air raid, when it may be too late.

Entrance and Exit.

Where possible two entrances, or a main entrance and an emergency exit, such as a window, should exist; they should be as far apart as possible, so that both are not likely to be blocked at the same time.

Independent Lighting.

As the normal source of electricity may be damaged, it is important to provide alternative means of lighting. In small shelters torches, or even candles and night-lights, may be used for alternative lighting.

Water Supply.

An adequate supply of drinking water should be available.

Flooding.

Steps should be taken where necessary to prevent the entry of rain water or water from mains damaged in a raid.

This may be done, for example, by provision of tide boards or by the heightening of parapets round the site of the shelter. Underground shelter accommodation should not be discarded solely on account of the fear of flooding, if means can be provided for the safe escape of its occupants.

An enlarged coal shute protected from debris can be arranged as an emergency exit from cellars.

Sanitary Arrangements.

For this purpose, chemical closets may be used if water closets are not available. Some provision, however, is essential.

Tools.

A number of tools such as picks, shovels, and crowbars should be kept in a shelter to be used in forcing a way out if the occupants are trapped. When the accommodation is being fitted out, it should be discovered where the weakest part of the structure is, or where it would be most suitable to work, should it become necessary to break a way out. This position should be clearly marked for the benefit of all.

Comforts and Occupation.

Chairs or other seating arrangements are required, and a table, if it can be accommodated, is desirable. Rugs and a stove will be found most welcome during night raids and in the winter months. A radio or gramophone, some books, table games, and toys where children are concerned, will also be found useful adjuncts to shelter equipment. The provision of a kettle, a safe means of boiling it, some tea or coffee, a few biscuits in tins and perhaps some tinned food in addition, will all help to make less irksome the time passed in the shelter.

It is important that persons in shelters should be given an occupation, preferably of the mind, since this will help to divert attention from the noise accompanying an air raid and to prevent idle speculations on what is going on outside. Vigorous activity in a shelter should be discouraged, since it increases the consumption of oxygen out of the air and unnecessarily raises the humidity.

If a dog is taken into the shelter, it is desirable that it should be muzzled.

Action to be taken on the Sounding of a Warning and Behaviour during an Air Raid.

It cannot be too strongly emphasised that it is most dangerous to give way to the temptation to watch what is going on in an air raid, and to remain out of doors or at a window instead of taking cover. Even if the raid is a considerable distance away, fragments of anti-aircraft shells may fall many miles from the scene of action, and in addition, with aircraft travelling at several miles a minute, a person watching a raid at some distance may find himself without warning in the middle of falling bombs. Owing to the great speed of modern aircraft, the bombs are released many miles before the target aimed at is reached, and the person who waits to see the bombers before taking cover may pay for his curiosity with his life.

When an air raid warning is heard, or the sound of gunfire or falling bombs is heard in the absence of any warning being sounded, it is of the utmost importance that everyone should seek cover at once, taking care that he has his respirator with him.

After a warning is sounded, the period before the raid begins is likely to be short. Persons in or near their own homes should betake themselves, with their dependents, in an orderly fashion, to the refuge; and employees at their place of business should take cover in the shelter provided. Those caught in the streets at the time of an air-raid warning should not attempt to go home, unless they can get there within five minutes. The local authorities, assisted by the Government, have provided public shelters for use by those persons for whom it would be unsafe to try to reach home. The presence of these shelters is clearly marked, and in congested areas they are situated at close intervals.

It is obvious that no time should be lost in finding the nearest shelter. This may not be difficult in daylight, but in the dark—perhaps on a moonless night—it might prove an almost hopeless task if no thought had been given to it beforehand. Signs are provided indicating the location of public shelters, and it should be made a matter of habit to look out, wherever one may be, for these notices, so that in case of sudden need arising to seek shelter no time may be lost in trying to find it.

Where persons are indoors on the announcement of an air raid, even where no refuge is provided, they should remain on the premises and should not make their way to a public shelter. Public shelters are provided for the safety of those who find themselves in the streets and far from home at the time of a raid. It is much safer to remain in an unprotected house than to be caught in the street when bombs are falling.

If a person in the street has not been able to find a public shelter before the raid begins, it is necessary to make the best use of any nearby buildings or other local features which can be turned to advantage as a means of providing cover. Partial protection from flying splinters and debris may be obtainable in archways, doorways, basement yards, under balconies, and against walls. Bodily contact with solid matter, such as with the wall of a basement area, a shelter, or a house, should be avoided since there is a danger of being hurt through the violent percussion or earth shock set up in the ground by the force of a bomb exploding nearby.

Protection of the lungs against blast can be secured to some extent by keeping the mouth slightly open, and this can best be done by gripping firmly between the teeth a piece of india rubber, a piece of soft wood, or a handkerchief rolled up tightly into a ball.

To protect the eardrums from shock it is useful to put a small pad of loosely packed cotton wool in the ears.

In the case of a bomb which penetrates the ground before exploding, the sides of the crater tend to confine the path of splinters to an upward direction, and even in the case of bombs which explode without penetration there is a zone of comparative safety near the ground. It is therefore safer to sit down than to stand up, and safer to lie than to sit. Thus, if a person finds himself in the open in an air raid and no shelter is available, he should lie flat, preferably in a ditch or in a fold of the ground, with face downwards, supporting his head in his folded arms. Protection should be given in any possible way to vital parts of the body against the fall of light objects.

The chart on page 22 gives an idea of the great reduction in the risk of injury which can be secured by acting on the simple precautions described.

After the Raid.

After the action warning has been sounded it is important not to emerge from the shelter until the " Raiders Passed " signal is given. It is even more important that an exit should not be made where gas has previously been announced by Warden's rattle until, in addition to the " Raiders Passed " message sounded by the siren, the " All Clear " is rung on Warden's handbells.

On emerging from shelter, it may often be the first impulse to wish to make inquiries by telephone as to how others in the vicinity have fared. This must not be done, since the communication system of the locality will certainly be required by the Civil Defence Authorities for the purpose of transmitting and receiving reports and for ordering out assistance to the scenes of damage, where the factor of time is of paramount importance. Those whose welfare is causing the most concern may unhappily be involved at a scene of damage, and the delay in getting help to them caused by unnecessary blockage of the lines of communication may be a deciding factor in their ultimate safety.

During a raid and, indeed, at all times in an emergency, it is necessary to keep calm, and to act swiftly, with the knowledge of the right course which must be gained beforehand.

When it is safe to do so after a raid, it is better to go out and help others than to stay at home and fret.

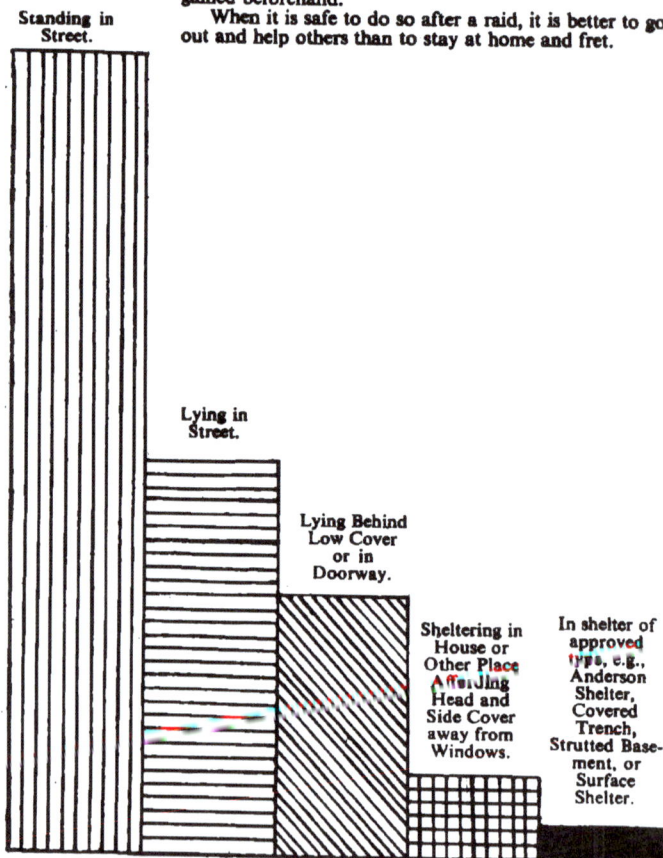

Standing in Street.

Lying in Street.

Lying Behind Low Cover or in Doorway.

Sheltering in House or Other Place Affording Head and Side Cover away from Windows.

In shelter of approved type, e.g., Anderson Shelter, Covered Trench, Strutted Basement, or Surface Shelter.

This diagram is based on a large number of reports of the results of recent air raids and is an approximate indication of the difference in the degree of risk resulting from taking cover in various ways.

CHAPTER 3.

INCENDIARY BOMBS.

Incendiary Bombs and Their Characteristics.

Incendiary Agents.

Many incendiary agents, such as petrol, thermite, phosphorus, and magnesium, have been used in war, but the most effective as a projectile is the Magnesium Bomb, which consists of a magnesium alloy exterior and a core of thermite priming composition.

The chief advantages of this type of bomb are that the whole of it is combustible with the exception of the striker mechanism and the sheet-iron tail fin, and that it remains active longer than most other forms of incendiary bomb of equal weight.

Incendiary Bomb Attack.

Generally speaking, the object of incendiary bomb attack from the air is to cause many fires over a large area at once. To do this each aircraft must carry as large a number as possible of the lightest bombs which will effectively start a fire; for this purpose the " kilo " or 2¼-lb. magnesium bomb offers great advantages since a large bomber can carry 1,000 or more of these bombs.

They may be released in salvos of 10 or 20, and if 15 per cent. of the bombs dropped in a normally built-up area actually hit buildings, a reasonable proportion for such an area, and only half of these started fires, at least 75 fires could be caused by a single aircraft.

If there were 10 aircraft 750 fires might thus be started simultaneously.

Penetration and Protection.

The light incendiary bomb has been designed to penetrate any ordinary roof material, such as slate or tile, and to become lodged in upper storeys, where a fire may result. Unless the bomb enters through a window, it will probably be arrested by the first boarded floor below the roof, where it will start a fire and then, burning its way through the floor, start a further fire on the floor below.

To lessen this risk, it is important to remove inflammable materials in attic or roof spaces. In addition, to prolong the resistance of woodwork to burning, it is helpful to apply liberally on upper roof timbers in these spaces one of the many recognised flame-resisting paints or plasters in accordance with the directions of the manufacturer. It is not difficult, however, and it is certainly far cheaper, to buy the ingredients of such a composition and prepare the mixture at home. For those who may wish to do so, the formula is :—

1¼ lb. of Kaolin (china clay) to 1 lb. 2 oz. of sodium silicate in syrup form, mixed in 1 pint of water.

It should be understood that the application of flame-resisting paints and plasters do not prevent fire, but simply prolong the resistance of dry woodwork to burning, thus giving the fire-fighter more time to get to the bomb before the surroundings are set alight. The resistance to burning in a floored roof space or attic can be greatly increased by covering the floor with 2 ins. of dry sand (if the ceiling structure will support the weight) or with some other suitable material.

Characteristics of Light Magnesium Bomb.

On impact the thermite core of the bomb is ignited and burns at a temperature sufficient to ignite the magnesium casing. In the initial period,

Typical Kilo Magnesium
Incendiary
Bomb.

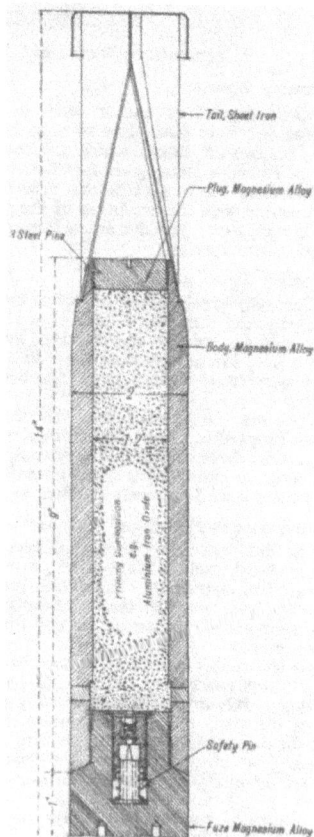

Typical Kilo Magnesium
Incendiary
Bomb—Sectional Drawing.

normally lasting about one minute, a violent spluttering takes place and molten incendiary matter is thrown a considerable distance, often about 30 ft. This may cause any inflammable material within reach to catch fire. After the initial stage the bomb will have become a small pool of molten magnesium, which will continue to burn with intense heat, but without spluttering, for about 10 minutes or more.

If left alone the magnesium will tend to trickle through floor boarding, burning its way as it goes, and so start further fires in the room below.

When, therefore, an incendiary bomb has penetrated a building, it becomes immediately necessary :—

(i) To subdue and localise the fire resulting from the bomb, since the main damage is caused by the fire;

(ii) To control the bomb and prevent it from burning through the floor.

Methods of Controlling the Bomb and Dealing with Incipient Fires.

The Use of Water.

The effect of applying water to burning magnesium is to increase the rate of burning by supplying oxygen, with the result that the bomb is rapidly burnt out.

Water should not, however, be thrown from a bucket or otherwise projected in quantity on a magnesium bomb, since this will cause very violent spluttering and scattering of the molten metal. Even a light jet of water will cause spluttering, and should not, therefore, be used on the bomb.

The best method of dealing with a magnesium bomb is by the application of water in a suitable spray, such as that produced by the stirrup hand pump; this enables the bomb to be dealt with at close quarters without any spluttering, and reduces the time of burning from about 10 minutes to a minute or so.

Stirrup Hand Pump.

The appliance specially recommended for dealing with incendiary bombs and the resultant fires is the stirrup hand pump. It is fitted with a dual-purpose nozzle which can produce either a spray or an $\frac{1}{4}$-in. jet of water as desired. The jet will normally carry effectively to a range of about 30 ft., and the spray to about 15 ft. It is supplied with 30 ft. of hose.

The advantages of the stirrup hand pump may be summarised as follows :

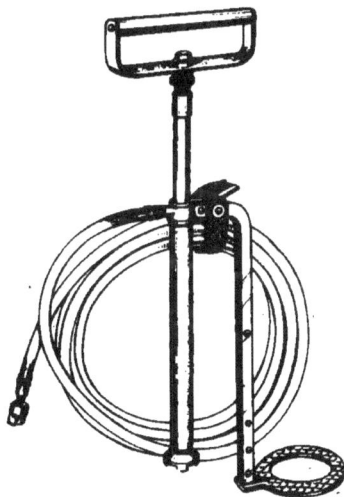

Stirrup Hand Pump.

25

(i) It provides within a single appliance a safe means of attacking both the fire and the bomb; the former with the spray, the latter with the jet. To change from a jet to spray it is necessary only to press a button in the base of the nozzle.

(ii) It enables the person operating the pump to keep well away from the intense heat and smoke.

(iii) It is economical in water consumption. Not more than 6 to 8 gallons of water are required to extinguish the bomb and any resultant fire in the room, provided the situation is tackled promptly.

(iv) It is a valuable means of fighting incipient domestic fires not necessarily resulting from incendiary bombs, and it may also be found to have other uses, for instance in the garden or garage.

Methods of Use.

The appliance may be operated effectively by two people, but three are preferable and they can best work as a team as follows :—

No. 1 takes charge of the fire-fighting and operates the nozzle at the end of the line of hose;

No. 2 pumps the water from a bucket at the other end of the hose;

No. 3 keeps the bucket replenished with water and relieves Nos. 1 and 2 as necessary.

No. 3 should also watch for the possible outbreak of fire in the floor below and in other likely places.

When the team consists of only two persons, the duties of No. 2 and No. 3 should be combined.

An independent source of water supply should be arranged in case water mains are damaged or the pressure of water in them is reduced owing to fire brigade activities elsewhere.

For this purpose, water should be stored beforehand in tanks or buckets, or used bath water may be retained in the bath during periods of heavy raiding.

To approach the fire without being overcome by smoke, fumes, and heat, No. 1 of the team should lie down and keep his face near the floor, where it will be found easier to breathe and to see. He should have a fireman's axe or light domestic hatchet conveniently available for dealing with obstacles in his approach to the bomb, and also an electric torch for use in the final search for smouldering remains. A wet blanket folded and slung across the left arm will help to provide protection against the heat and against spluttering magnesium.

Sequence of Action.

After the initial period of intense spluttering, the situation should be tackled as follows :—

(i) The fire caused by the bomb should normally be controlled first by means of the jet. Until this has been done the operator may not be able to approach the bomb sufficiently closely to direct the spray upon it.

(ii) The spray should then be directed on the bomb, and during this period the operator should gradually work nearer to the bomb so that he is finally attacking it from 6 ft. He should continue to direct the spray upon the bomb until it is entirely consumed, but it may be necessary to stop spraying the bomb occasionally so as to keep the resultant fire under control with the jet.

Controlling Fire with Jet.

Directing Spray on the Bomb.

Shovelling Sand on the Bomb.

(iii) As soon as the bomb is extinct, the operator should extinguish any burning parts which remain in the surrounding space.

(iv) As there is danger of fire creeping into unseen places where it may remain unnoticed in a smouldering condition, a thorough search must be made; for this purpose it may be necessary to lift floor boards or to remove panelling and skirting from the walls.

Alternative Methods.

Where an incendiary bomb is found burning upon an incombustible surface, such as the tiled or concrete floor of a kitchen or scullery, an

The Bomb Almost Completely Controlled by Sand.

alternative technique may be used if the surrounding area has not already been set alight. The principle of this technique is to control the combustion by smothering the bomb with dry sand. A close approach can then be made and the bomb may safely be scooped into a receptacle containing a few inches of sand and so removed outside.

The best appliances for use with this method are the Redhill container and long-handled scoop and hoe. The container should be kept full with dry sand and situated together with the scoop and hoe conveniently near the place where it may have to be used.

If no other appliances are available, a bucket or coal-scuttle, and a shovel or garden spade, may serve the purpose, provided that a supply of sand, earth, or domestic ash is readily accessible, with which to smother the bomb and to provide a protective layer of a few inches thickness in the base of the improvised container. When the bomb is completely smothered, it may be scooped into the container and removed, care being taken to scoop up every particle of burning molten metal.

Use of Chemical Extinguishers.

Many chemical extinguishers are excellent for the purpose for which they have been designed, but would have certain disadvantages in meeting the situation caused by an incendiary bomb.

The average soda-acid extinguisher is of the 2-gallon type. A single extinguisher of this type would not, as a general rule, be capable of dealing with the bomb and the resultant fire. In addition, it would be difficult to handle when thick smoke made it necessary for the fire-fighter to keep close to the ground.

Some extinguishers designed for special purposes would actually be dangerous; for example, carbon tetrachloride, which is used in some, generates phosgene, a poisonous gas, when in contact with the burning magnesium.

Larger Fires.

If an incendiary bomb is not dealt with quickly, a serious fire may result and the situation will probably call for the resources of the organised fire service. In order to prevent the spread of fires, it is essential that the fire service, if required, should be called without delay. It is of vital importance, therefore, that everyone should know the fire organisation in his locality and the quickest way of obtaining assistance. Telephone lines and fire alarms may well be congested or out of order, and it would be wise to have a notice pinned up near the door stating where the nearest fire station or auxiliary fire station is or the route followed by the fire patrols.

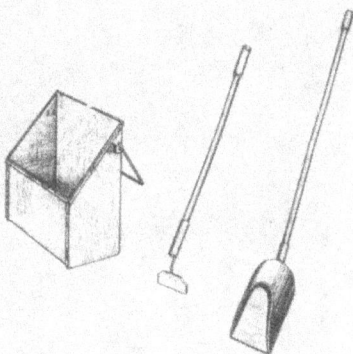

The Redhill Container. The Long-handled Scoop and Hoe. These are joined together for shovelling sand on the bomb, as shown in the illustration on page 28.

In addition, the following notes may be found useful by householders for dealing with a situation where a serious fire has been started.

(a) In searching a house for occupants, a start should be made at the top and continued downwards.

(b) To avoid smoke and heat, a person should lie down and crawl with head low. This method applies equally to life-saving and fire-fighting.

(c) Doors and windows must be kept closed to restrict the supply of fresh air to the fire. The door of a room in which there is believed to be a fire should not be opened until appliances are ready and in position to attack the fire.

(*d*) Passages or stairways on fire should not be used if rescue from outside can be effected through the window.

(*e*) When using stairways and passages, or crossing rooms, a person should keep near the walls where there is greater support for the floor.

(*f*) If the door of a burning room opens outwards, it is important to control its swing by placing the foot a few inches back from the closed door, so that it may be opened steadily and used as a shield for the body against the outrush of flame and smoke which might otherwise overcome the person about to enter. After this a prone position should be adopted.

Opening the Door of a Burning Room.

(*g*) To move an insensible person, the body should be laid with the face uppermost and the wrists tied together. The rescuer should then kneel astride the body and insert his head through the loop of the arms thus tied, and crawl.

31

Rescuing an Insensible Person from a Burning Room.

Bringing an Insensible Person Downstairs.

Smothering the Flames when Clothing is on Fire.

To move the body downstairs, it should be placed face uppermost with the head down the stairs. The rescuer should then lead downstairs by crawling backwards, helping the body down with his hands placed under the armpits.

(*h*) If a person's clothing is on fire, he should clap his hands over his mouth, lie down and roll.

If the clothing of another is on fire, the rescuer should make him lie down with the burning part uppermost. He should then approach the victim, holding in front of himself a blanket, rug, overcoat, or any other article suitable for smothering the flames, and cover the flames with the material. The victim should then be rolled until the flames have been put out.

(*i*) To escape from a window without a rope, the proper procedure is to sit on the sill, turn round, lower the body to the full extent of the arms, and then drop with the knees bent, endeavouring to spring slightly away from the walls.

Preparing to Escape from an Upstairs Window.

Dropping from an Upstairs Window.

Precautions to be Taken in Advance

Fire brigades throughout the country have been augmented for the purpose of dealing with incendiary bomb attack. But in spite of this the fire brigade services might be severely strained in the event of a heavy incendiary bomb attack and water for their use may temporarily cease to be available locally owing to heavy demands elsewhere.

It is therefore of vital importance that as many of the public as possible should be in a position to deal with fires on their own property before they become unmanageable; there is no household in which this can be neglected with impunity.

The following are the more important precautions which should be taken in advance in order to deal with incendiary bombs :—

(1) In every household, each adult should be made familiar with the methods of tackling both the bomb and the resultant fire, and duties should be allotted to each person in advance.

(2) The appropriate appliances should be obtained before they are required; the cost of doing so may often conveniently be shared between neighbouring households. Supplies of water, independent of the mains, and of sand or dry earth, should always be ready to hand.

and everyone should know where these supplies and any stirrup hand pump or other appliance which is available are to be found.

(3) Preliminary drill is essential; each person should practise the special duties which he has undertaken to perform, and when he is proficient he should also practise the duties of others, so that each may be interchangeable with the other.

(4) Spaces under the roof, such as attics, in which incendiary bombs are most likely to lodge, should be cleared of combustible material beforehand, and ready access to attics and roof spaces should be provided and made known to the persons concerned.

It should be constantly borne in mind that every incendiary bomb which is promptly brought under control, besides saving water supplies which may be of vital importance for dealing with major fires, averts the risk of a conflagration which may end with the extensive destruction of property and life.

CHAPTER 4.

WAR GASES.

The Nature of War Gases.

The term " gas," in reference to warfare, covers any chemical substance, whether solid, liquid, or vapour, used to produce poisonous or irritant effects upon the human body. A war gas may be used by itself or in combination with other gases so that the presence of any one of them may be masked and its identification made more difficult.

Gases are generally classified in two main categories : non-persistent and persistent.

Non-persistent Gas.

Non-persistent gases are so called because, in whatever form they are released, they are almost instantly converted into gas or smoke which is gradually dissipated by dilution with the atmosphere when the air is in movement. They are effective, therefore, for only a comparatively short time except when there is no air movement, in which case the process of dilution with the surrounding atmosphere is impeded, and the gas remains effective for a longer period.

Some non-persistent gases are visible at the point of release, and wherever the concentration is sufficiently high.

Persistent Gas.

Persistent gases are usually liberated in the form of liquids, and are called persistent because the process of conversion of the liquid into vapour is prolonged; the liquid itself is dangerous to touch, and any area on which it has fallen will continue to give off vapour in dangerous concentrations until the liquid has completely evaporated or been removed or neutralised.

The vapour of persistent gas is normally invisible, and like non-persistent gases, drifts with the wind, gradually becoming dissipated by dilution the further it moves from the source.

Effects of War Gases on the Body.

War gases may also be classified by their effects on the body to form two general categories, non-blister and blister.

Non-blister gases may further be classified as follows.

Lung Irritants (Choking Gases).

In dangerous concentrations these gases immediately produce smarting and watering of the eyes, irritation of the throat, and violent coughing and retching (this is specially marked with chlorine and chloropicrin). Breathing strong concentrations of them, even for a very short time, may cause death. Phosgene is one of the most deadly of these gases.

Lung irritants are usually non-persistent gases.

Eye Irritants (Tear Gases).

These gases, even in low concentrations, cause extreme smarting and watering of the eyes. Their effects are only temporary and pass off soon after withdrawal from the affected area or after the respirator is put on. They are effective as harassing agents and might be employed to cause panic and threaten morale.

Tear gases may be either persistent or non-persistent. Their appearance in liquid form is similar to that of blister gas, and they may be mixed with this type of gas in order to mask its presence.

Nose Irritants (Sneezing Gases).

These gases are non-persistent, and consist of solid arsenical compounds liberated as very fine particles in the form of a dust or " smoke." They are generally invisible except near the source, and have practically no smell. They produce intense irritation and pain in the nose, mouth, throat, and chest, which is often accompanied by sneezing and headaches.

These effects may be slightly delayed, and in severe cases may be accompanied by feelings of acute mental distress. As immediate relief is not felt after the respirator has been put on, a false belief may arise that the appliance is failing in its purpose. This, and the nauseating effect of the gas, will create a strong impulse to discard the respirator, which in no circumstances should be permitted. The effects will normally pass off quickly if the respirator has been promptly put on and kept on. Permanent injury is most unlikely to be caused by this type of gas.

Blister Gases.

These gases, whether in the form of liquid or vapour, have the effect of burning and blistering the skin, and may cause injuries to any part of the body which will take long to heal. In both liquid and vapour form they will readily penetrate ordinary clothing. Prolonged exposure to the vapour will cause injury to the eyes and the entry of liquid into the eyes may even cause blindness. If the vapour is inhaled in large quantities or contaminated food eaten, serious internal injuries may be caused. Nevertheless, short exposure to a low concentration of blister gas vapour need have no ill effects.

The two most important blister gases are mustard gas and lewisite. Mustard gas is the better known of these and, unlike lewisite, it produces no immediately noticeable effects on contact or inhalation, and so the need for protection against it may not be appreciated until it is too late. If liquid enters the eye, however, this would immediately be felt.

Contamination.

The word contamination has been adopted to imply the pollution of any substance by war gas in any form, whether solid, liquid, or vapour. This contamination, which is of particular importance in the case of blister gas, is insidious and far-reaching in its effects. Both the liquid and the vapour are absorbed by all porous substances which, when contaminated, continue both to be dangerous to touch and also to give off poisonous vapour after all visible evidence of contamination may have disappeared. Any person touching or walking on a contaminated surface becomes contaminated and would not only suffer injury himself but would carry contamination elsewhere. Likewise contamination may be spread by animals or vehicles.

Foodstuffs which have been subjected to blister gas in any form become agents of contamination, and as such are dangerous; in the worse cases they will have to be destroyed.

Gas Attacks.

One way in which gas can be released from aircraft is by being dropped in bombs. The casing of a gas bomb is usually of thin material, and may contain a small explosive charge sufficient to burst it and release the gas. The sound of the explosion is only slight as compared to that of a high explosive bomb of similar weight, and so normally it would not be mistaken. On the bursting of the bomb, a dangerous concentration of vapour is produced and a considerable area around the point of burst will also be made dangerous by splashes of the liquid.

Persistent gas can also be released in the form of spray from a container in the aircraft. From a low altitude the spray of liquid gas would be heavy, but the area covered by the spray from one aeroplane would be limited to a comparatively narrow zone corresponding to the path of flight and the direction of the wind. Spray from high altitudes would fall upon a much larger area, but owing to its fineness when it reaches the ground it would be of little effect except when it fell directly on to human beings.

Behaviour of Gas.

The effectiveness of gas is markedly influenced by the characteristics of the area in which it is used, and by the weather conditions prevailing at the time.

Unlike coal gas, war gases are generally heavier than air, it being an important requirement that they shall remain near to the ground where they will be effective and that they shall not be too rapidly dissipated by dilution. Consequently they will normally tend to remain longer on low-lying ground in hollows such as the basement areas of houses, where, to a large extent, they will be sheltered from the dissipating effects of the surrounding air movements.

The principal weather conditions affecting the behaviour of gases are wind, temperature, and rain.

The effect of wind is to carry gas along with it and to accelerate the rate of dispersal. In the case of a persistent gas, the liquid continues to give off dangerous vapour, but the local concentration is lower than it would be in the absence of wind. In built-up areas the free movement of air is to some extent restricted, and consequently gas will tend to remain in these areas longer than elsewhere.

Temperature chiefly affects persistent gases. In warm weather the danger from vapour is increased. If it is sufficiently cold, the liquid will freeze and become solid; there will be little danger from vapour while the gas is in a frozen condition, but in the case of blister gases direct contact with the frozen liquid, or with any contaminated object which is frozen, will still produce skin burns.

Light rain has little effect upon gases, but heavy rain tends to wash gas out of the air, and to wash away and destroy any liquid gas lying upon the ground or other exposed surface.

Non-persistent gas is thus most dangerous when used in calm, dry weather, and persistent gas in dry weather with a high ground temperature and a light breeze; and the danger of both is further increased in a built-up area.

Where there is any movement of air, the areas affected by the gas will be downwind from the point of burst. It is most important, therefore, that persons who find themselves in the open in the presence of gas should immediately make their way diagonally upwind, so as to reach an area of safety beyond the point of release. They should, of course, not walk towards the point of release where the concentration will be greatest, but move laterally out of the path of travel of the gas.

Respirators for the General Public.

Respirators have been issued by the Government to the whole population. They are the property of the Crown, and as such they may not be maltreated or used for any purpose other than that for which they are intended. It is essential that they shall be worn by everyone who comes within range of war gases dropped by the enemy except those within gasproof shelter.

These respirators will give protection to the eyes and lungs under any conditions likely to arise from the use of any war gas in air raids. None of them is designed to protect the wearer against domestic and other noxious gases which are not used in warfare.

There are three principal types of civilian respirator designed to suit the different ages of wearer. They are the General Civilian Respirator, the Small Child's Respirator for children from about 4 years down to 18 months, and the Anti-gas Helmet for Babies, designed for infants in arms.

The Civilian Respirator.

Description. This respirator has a window of non-inflammable transparent material let into a facepiece of thin sheet rubber which covers the eyes, nose, and mouth, and which is held in position by head-harness. To this facepiece is attached a container which holds activated charcoal to absorb gases from the incoming air, and a filter to prevent the passage of the fine particles of poisonous smokes; the standard of protection against these smokes is now being improved by the fitting of an additional filter known as Contex. Those areas in which Contex filters have not already been supplied will receive them in due course. The local authorities will notify the public when they are available. The fitting of Contex should be carried out only by wardens or other A.R.P. officials.

Thrusting the Chin into the Civilian
Respirator.

Adjusting the Civilian
Respirator.

39

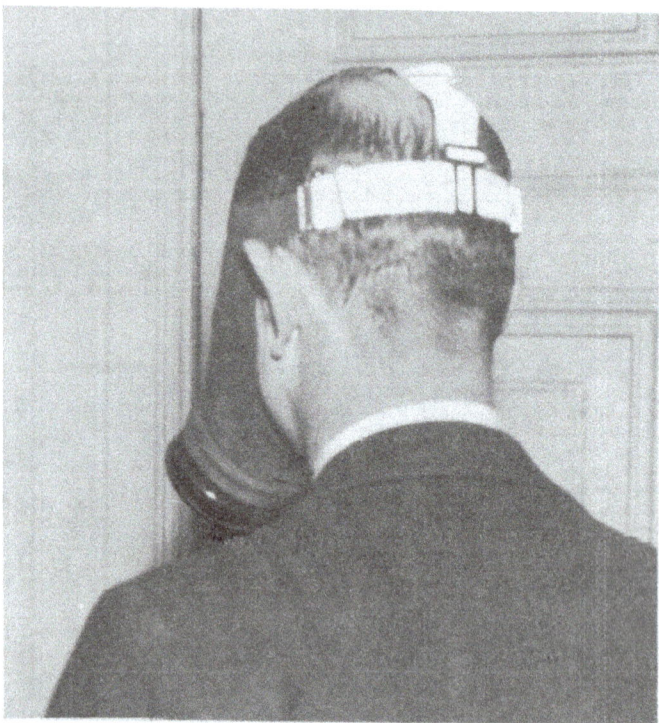

Back of the Head with Respirator in Position,shewing central position of buckle.

Air is drawn in through the container, and the exhaled air is prevented from passing back through the same channel by a simple non-return valve consisting of a flat rubber disc attached to the inner end of the container. The exhaled air forces its way out by lifting the thin rubber of the facepiece at its edges, so that a separate outlet valve is unnecessary.

The facepiece of this respirator is provided in three sizes—" Small," " Medium," and " Large "—and the size is marked on the head-straps, or moulded on the brow of the facepiece. The same container is fitted to all sizes.

The " Small " size of the civilian respirator will normally fit a child from 4 years upwards, but in many cases it may be found that a child is sufficiently developed below this age to be likewise accommodated.

A stout cardboard carton is provided, and when not in use the respirator should always be kept in this or in one of the types of carrier referred to later.

Putting on. Before putting on the respirator it is first necessary to stop breathing and remove any headdress. The respirator should be held in front of the face by each of the side straps with the thumbs under the straps; the chin should be thrust into the facepiece, the straps being drawn over the head as far as they will comfortably reach. The breath should then be released in order to expel any gas inside the facepiece, and normal breathing resumed. The headdress may then be replaced.

Spectacles or pince-nez must always be removed before the respirator is put on since they will interfere with the fit and so admit poison gas.

Adjusting. If the respirator is properly adjusted it should be quite comfortable in use, and provide a gastight fit in all positions of the head. If the rubber facepiece is stretched too tightly it will be uncomfortable because of the pressure on the face and the undue resistance to the exhaled air, which must pass between the rubber facepiece and the face, usually at the cheeks. This resistance to breathing will be found most exhausting, and the defect may be overcome either by the fitting of a larger size of respirator, if it is not already the large size, or by the proper manipulation of the adjustable head-harness.

Testing Fit. If the fit is too loose or incorrect, air may be breathed in without passing through the purifying materials held in the container. This can be tested by holding a flat surface, such as a piece of paper or cardboard or a cork mat, against the outer end of the container, and attempting to inhale. If the intake of air is found to be impossible and the facepiece is sucked in against the cheeks, it can be assumed that a gastight fit is provided.

If Contex has been fitted, a piece of stiff paper or card will not seal the holes, because the end of the Contex is corrugated. A thin cellophane jam jar cover may be used instead, or a piece of very thin, good-quality paper.

Size. The correct size of respirator can be judged by the position of the transparent window in relation to the eyes, which should be on a line about midway between the upper and lower edges of the panel. If the eyes are considerably above this line, the respirator is too small; if they are much below, it is too large.

Preparing to Remove the Civilian Respirator.

Checking. In making tests, and always when wearing the respirator, it must be ensured that the edges of the rubber facepiece are not doubled under and that the straps are not twisted. The buckle should be centred at the back at the crown of the head and the facepiece should be straight on the face with the two side straps horizontal.

Women should adjust their hair so that it does not lie under the facepiece, and it may also be necessary to remove hairpins to ensure a safe and comfortable fit.

Securing. When the correct adjustment of the head-straps has been found, the safety-pins provided should be used to ensure that it is maintained. In the case of children, to make sure that the respirator remains comfortable,

41

adjustments may be necessary from time to time, in accordance with the growth of the child.

Removal. To remove the respirator, the thumb should be inserted under the buckle at the back of the head and the straps drawn forward over the top of the head and then in a downward direction. Any other method may cause damage to the facepiece, and must not be attempted.

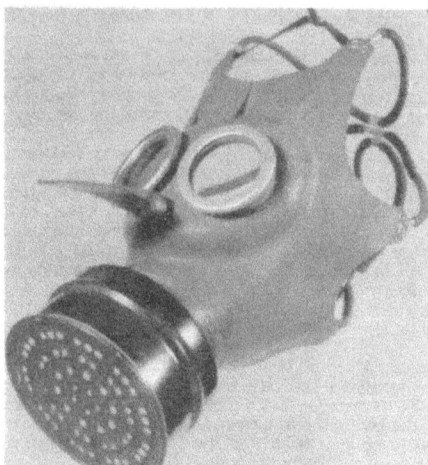

The Small Child's Respirator.

Children do not, as a general rule, take well to wearing respirators, and the difficulties their parents and guardians may have in this connection, together with the other dangers of air raids, should be avoided where possible by the evacuation of children from the more vulnerable areas. The possibility of air raids, even in the comparatively safe reception areas, cannot, however, be wholly discounted, and the Government have therefore made a general distribution of the Small Child's Respirator.

Description. An attempt has been made in the design of this respirator to make it as acceptable as possible to young children. The colours have been made attractive; it has been made as light in weight as possible; the head-harness will not weaken in use, is gentle in its pull on the facepiece, and is so designed that it prevents the respirator from being easily pulled off. Since the child breathes much less air than an adult, a less bulky and lighter container than that of the ordinary Civilian Respirator has been included, and this is screwed into the facepiece.

The container causes only a negligible resistance to the child's breathing, and the air breathed out passes out of the facepiece through a soft rubber valve which opens freely under the pressure of the breath. Contex may be added to this container also.

The facepiece is made of soft rubber so that it readily takes the shape of the child's face and makes close contact with the skin. Eyepieces are fitted in place of the transparent window found in the Civilian Respirator.

Putting on and Removal. The respirator is put on in the same way as the adult respirator. Many children quickly learn to put it on themselves if they are shown how to thrust the chin forward into it. If it is put on by a second person it is better to do so from behind, with the back of the child's head resting against the chest of the adult, so that the child's neck is supported against the action of pulling the spring harness over the head. To remove the respirator, it should first be unhooked at the back of the head, and the

Small Child's Respirator.

42

instructions for putting it on then reversed, the movements following closely those given for the removal of the adult type.

Adjustment and Testing. The head-harness is suitable for all sizes of heads without adjustment. If the respirator is properly put on with the harness secured by means of the hook and eye at the back, the fit of the respirator is automatically ensured if the child's face is of the correct size for it, and the close contact between the rubber and the face can clearly be seen. It is unnecessary, therefore, to test for gas-tightness, as suggested in the case of the Civilian Respirator, and this is not recommended.

There is only one size of Small Child's Respirator. If there is difficulty in stretching the head harness over the head, or the eyes are unduly high in the eyepieces, this type of respirator is too small for the child, and a small Civilian type should be used. If the facepiece of the Small Child's Respirator puckers at the edges or is loose on the face, or the eyes are unduly low in the eyepieces, the child is too small for this type, and the special appliance, known as the Baby's Anti-Gas Protective Helmet, should be used.

The Baby's Protective Helmet.

Infants in arms up to the age of about 18 months and young children who show a marked distaste for the Small Child's Respirator, or are otherwise temperamentally or physically unfitted to wear this type, may be accommodated by the Baby's Helmet.

Description. It consists of a hood, made of impervious fabric and fitted with a large window, which encloses the head, shoulders, and arms, and is closed around the waist by means of a draw tape. A baby, when in it, is thus able to get its hand to its mouth. The hood is surrounded by and fastened to a light metal frame, which is lengthened on the underside and fitted with a tail-piece which can be adjusted by means of two screws turned with a coin, so as to form a support and protection for the baby's back. The length should be such that the baby's face is opposite the middle of the window. It can be made extra long, if required, by overlapping the tailpiece on the last two screw holes only and using an extra screw and nut in the hole which has no fixed nut. A spare screw and nut for this purpose will be found on the domed top of the frame.

The tailpiece is turned up at the end to form a seat which prevents the occupant from slipping out of the hood. The baby is made secure in the helmet by means of a T-shaped supporting strap connected to the end of the tailpiece. The metal frame and supporting strap may be varied in length to suit all sizes of babies and children up to about 5 years of age.

The hood is padded on the underside where the baby rests. Padding has been omitted from the tailpiece since babies are likely to soil any padding in this position. If required, mothers can supply some washable padding, e.g., a folded towel or napkin, for this part of the frame.

Folding legs are provided on the metal frame for use when the helmet is not being carried or nursed. The legs will prevent the helmet from rolling over if it is laid down with a child in it, and they are for use when a baby is being put into the helmet.

Air is supplied to the inside of the hood by means of a rubber bellows placed conveniently for the right hand. The air passes through a container which removes all poison gas from it, and enters the hood at the top through a specially shaped orifice which deflects the air upwards so that it sweeps out all vitiated air from the hood and also prevents the stream of air from blowing directly on the baby's head. A slow and steady rate of pumping of about 40 strokes a minute is adequate for keeping out gas and supplying enough purified air even for a child of 4-5 years of age. The space in the hood is large

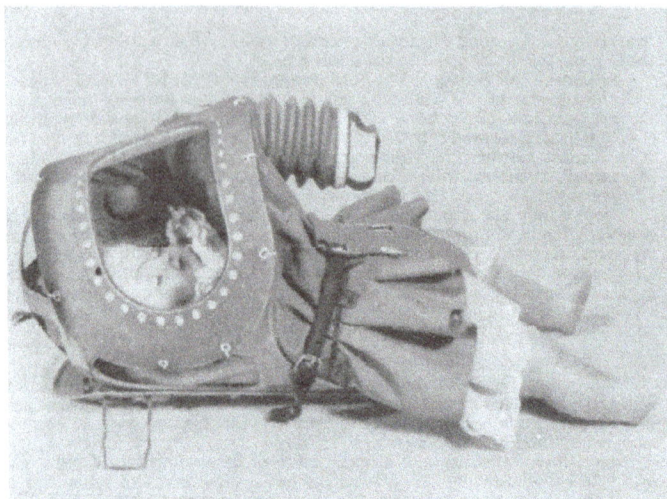

Baby's Anti-Gas Helmet.

enough to allow pumping to be stopped for several minutes if required without causing discomfort. When pumping, the operator should be careful not to obstruct the intake holes which lie in the disc at the movable end of the bellows under the palm of the hand.

There is no limit to the time during which a child may remain in the helmet if steady pumping is maintained.

Contex may be fitted to the container in a baby's helmet, but only by properly qualified persons. The helmet should never be taken to pieces by an unskilled person because there is a risk of its being reassembled wrongly, so that it will not protect the baby against gas.

Fitting and Operation. To put the baby into the helmet it is necessary to proceed as follows :—

(1) The wire legs of the helmet should be opened and clicked back.

(2) The helmet should be laid down with the skirt of the bag open and the top turned back over the window. The wide strap attached to the turned-up end of the metal tailpiece should be out of the way, so that the baby will not lie upon it.

(3) The baby should be placed in the helmet so that its seat rests in the curve of the tailpiece with one leg on each side.

(4) The skirt should then be pulled down over the baby and it should be ensured that both arms are free and are put up inside the bag before the tape is tied. The ends should then be drawn snugly, but not too tightly, around the infant's waist, and finally finished off by tying in a bow.

(5) The supporting piece should now be brought up between the legs and the ends of the canvas strap attached to the buckles on each side of

the frame so as to hold the baby firmly in place. If the frame is being used in one of the shorter positions of adjustment, it may be necessary to shorten the supporting piece in order to hold the child securely. This may be done by folding down the top end either once or twice, as required, and passing the ends of the canvas strap out through the metal slots.

(6) When the baby has thus been safely secured in the helmet, the bellows should be operated. First, at least twelve sharp strokes are required to clear out the air in the helmet, and then a slow and steady rate should be maintained.

The baby in its bag can be nursed on the lap or carried in the arms in the normal way; if it must be taken some distance, the legs of the frame should be folded underneath, and a wide shawl used as a sling to support the baby from the mother's shoulders.

It is desirable that the complete drill described should be practised both in daylight and in darkness, and when the parent or guardian is herself wearing a respirator.

Since the growth of infants is sometimes rapid, frequent adjustments may be necessary to the length of the helmet in order that the child may at all times be comfortable and fully protected.

The carton in which the baby's helmet is supplied is only large enough, with the normal method of packing, to take the helmet with the tailpiece unextended, and the extension of the tailpiece to keep pace with the baby's growth will therefore present a problem from the point of view of packing. It is desirable that the helmet should be kept with the tailpiece extended to the proper length, and at the same time it is important to avoid mutilation of the carton, in view of the need for economy of cardboard. The following method of packing, which will be demonstrated to parents of babies by wardens, should therefore be used when it is necessary to extend the tailpiece of the helmet.

The flap of one end of the carton should be turned down inside the carton and the helmet inserted upside down in the carton with the extended tailpiece sticking out over the end of the turned-down flap. The other end-flap should then be closed and the side-flaps closed over the top, a piece of string being tied round the whole carton. The carton will then enclose the whole helmet and keep it reasonably free from light and dust, even though the end of the tailpiece protrudes at one end.

Use and Care of Respirators.

On all occasions when gas is present and a gas-protected room or refuge is not available or has to be vacated, the respirator must be put on without delay. In order to ensure this it is necessary to take the respirator on all journeys on which the wearer will be more than five minutes away from the place where it is ordinarily kept. It is also necessary to practise putting on and taking off the respirator both by daylight and in darkness, so that this may be done when required with the minimum delay. Furthermore, it is desirable to become accustomed to the wearing of a respirator, and to be sure that the respirator is comfortable in practical use over a period of time, since it must not be removed for adjustment in the actual presence of gas.

After use, whether for practice or otherwise, the inside of the facepiece or bag should always be wiped dry before the respirator is returned to its carrier. If wet from exposure to rain the outside should also be wiped.

Occasionally it may be necessary to clean the appliance more thoroughly. This may be done by means of a small sponge or soft cloth dipped in a rich solution of toilet soap and lukewarm water and wrung out thoroughly before

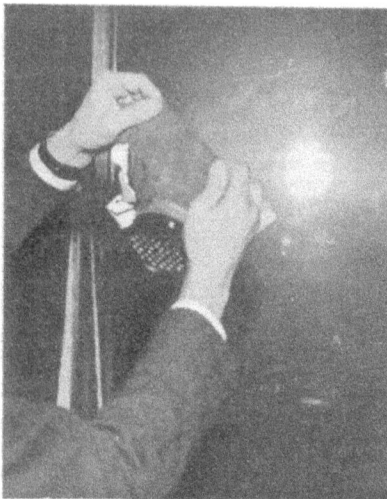

Testing Rubber of Mask.

swabbing. The appliance should then be sponged in the same way with clean water, well wrung out. Great care must be taken, however, to prevent the entry of any moisture into the container, since this will damage its contents and impair its efficiency.

Respirators of all types should always be put away quite dry. Those of the general civilian type should be folded in such a way as to prevent kinking or unduly bending the delicate transparent window. All respirators should be kept in a cool, dry place, away from a strong light or heat; they should never be left in front of a fire, near a radiator, or in the sun. Respirators other than the baby's helmet should not be carried or hung suspended from the straps, nor should they be confined to their carrier for long periods without being taken out periodically, since this may affect the fit through prolonged distortion of the facepiece.

Occasional inspections should be carried out by the holders of respirators to make sure that they are in good condition, but it must be stressed that any undue tampering with the delicate sections is likely to do more harm than good.

The following are a few general points, applicable in particular to the general civilian respirator, which should be looked at occasionally; if any faults are disclosed the local warden should immediately be consulted :—

The transparent window is the most easily damaged part, and cracks or weaknesses should be looked for by holding before a light. The stitching round the edges must be secure. At the same time the thin rubber of the facepiece can be tested for punctures, tears, and signs of perishing, by gently stretching it so that a section of an inch is expanded to about 2 inches. Chafing caused by friction against the sides of the carrier, especially where this is not of the Government pattern, is almost always responsible for any weaknesses detected here.

The thin rubber disc fitted centrally to the valve pin on the inside end of the metal container should be soft, pliable, and flat. If it is concave it should be taken off the pin and reversed. If it has hardened, it should be renewed.

The rubber band joining the facepiece of the general civilian respirator to the metal container should be perfectly fresh and elastic. If it shows cracks, it is perishing and should be renewed. Stitching generally should be sound. The container of the Small Child's Respirator screws into the facepiece; it should be ensured that this is tightly done up.

46

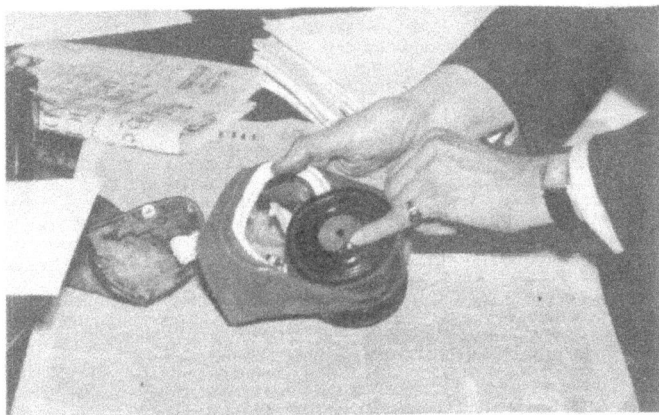

Examining Rubber Disc.

A severely dented container, or one which is perforated, or into which moisture has entered (as may be detected by the discolouration of the white filter material visible through the air holes at the outer end of the container), should be further examined by a competent official of the local A.R.P. organisation.

In all cases, whether further advice or a new part of a respirator is required, the local warden should be consulted.

Treatment to Prevent Misting of Eyepieces.

When respirators are worn, moisture from the breath will condense inside them and vision will tend to be obstructed by misting of the transparent window or eyepieces. This can be avoided by the application of a thin film of toilet soap lightly smeared with the finger upon the inside of the window.

It is suggested that this treatment should always be applied on putting the respirator away after use so that it will be immediately ready to put on when required. If the respirator is not worn, the treatment remains effective for a week, after which time the window should be lightly sponged and dried, and a fresh treatment applied.

Carriers for the Civilian and Small Child's Respirators.

Respirators should be kept and carried in the cardboard carton provided for them. They should be inserted with the container leading; the container of the Civilian Respirator should be inserted into the recess at the bottom of the carton, the facepiece being folded over so that the transparent eyepiece lies evenly on the top of the container at full length, without any deformation.

In order to preserve the carton and to protect it from rain, it is recommended that it should be enclosed in a waterproof satchel, or other durable form of cover, fitted with a suitable shoulder strap. The satchel should be so designed that rain cannot enter between the flap and the body, and so that access to the respirator is impeded as little as possible. For instance, the flap

47

should be secured by means of press studs and not by tie-tapes, which might be difficult to untie in a hurry, and the flap of the satchel should be positioned so as to coincide with the lid of the carton.

No other article of any description, such as first-aid outfit, electric torch, anti-gas ointment, lipstick, face-powder, etc., must be carried in the carton with the respirator. If, for convenience, it is desired to combine carriage of such articles with that of the respirator, provision must be made for them in separate pockets or compartments in the satchel.

If no satchel or cover is used, the cardboard carton can be strengthened at the bottom joint, at the corners and the hinge of the lid with adhesive tape. The carrying cord should be threaded outside the bottom of the carton to prevent the bottom slipping loose. The water-resistance of the carton can be improved by painting it, on the outside only, with any good-quality oil paint. In rain the carton, if not provided with a waterproof cover, should be carried under the coat or mackintosh.

Alternative forms of carrier to the official carton may be purchased, but great care must be exercised before using such alternatives that no damage or deterioration of the respirator is likely to ensue. The following general principles must be observed when choosing a carrier :—

(1) The carrier must be designed and made of material which is sufficiently rigid to protect the respirator from being crushed, e.g., in a dense crowd, or against a seat in a moving omnibus, or if the carrier is dropped to the ground.

(2) The carrier must have a smooth interior with no inward projection, such as a rim, lip, or sharp rivet head, which would either scratch or catch against the edge of the eyepiece during insertion, withdrawal, or ordinary carriage of the respirator.

(3) The respirator must not be a very loose fit in the carrier, so that it rattles and gradually abrades the rubber around the container.

(4) The carrier must be of such a size and shape that it neither causes nor allows gross distortion of the facepiece, e.g., it must not require the facepiece to be turned inside out, or be such that the container either rests or can become inverted on to the facepiece.

(5) If the carrier forms part of a hold-all, e.g., if combined with a shopping bag or a handbag, it must allow of direct and rapid access to the respirator without the necessity of first removing other articles.

Gasproof Accommodation.

In view of the universal provision of respirators, gasproof accommodation in the ordinary house is not essential, but where it is possible to do so it is an advantage to make the refuge or shelter gasproof. The main principle to be observed in this connection is the blockage of all sources of draught into the room. Such places as the fireplace or ventilator gratings in the walls

Civilian Respirator Correctly Packed in Carton.

encourage draught, and consequently it is difficult to prevent the entry of air (and gas, if present) under doorways, between the floorboards, through cracks in walls, and, where windows have not been bricked in, between frames and window, unless these natural ventilators are first blocked. If this is done, quite simple means, such as pasting layers of brown paper over cracks in walls and flooring and over gratings and plugging other places with tightly rolled newspaper or pieces of felt, will answer the purpose adequately, and no undue expense or preparation is consequently necessary.

Whether or not a gasproof refuge is available, the respirator must always be taken there during air raids, since even the distant effects of blast from H.E. bombs may destroy the gas-tightness of the chamber, and if gas were used the respirator would then immediately be required.

Where the provision of gas-tightness in a refuge renders the room otherwise untenable for ordinary use, and so presents a source of difficulty or embarrassment to the householder, it is suggested that the materials required for the purpose be immediately obtained and left in the refuge, but that they need not be applied until it is clear that the enemy propose to use gas against this country in air raids or they have already done so. At such a time there should be no further delay in completing the preparations.

Generally, when gas is announced in an area by the warden's rattle, if no gasproof accommodation is available, or the gas-tightness of a refuge has been destroyed by the effects of the raid, respirators should immediately be put on. Normally they need be kept on only until the warden's handbell announces the region "All Clear" and free of gas. But if gas has penetrated the building, it will be necessary to clear this by adequate ventilation, employing means of forcing the air to circulate freely throughout the building, so that the premises can be made safe for normal habitation without the use of respirators. In spite of the sounding of handbells, therefore, respirators, when worn, should not be taken off until it is certain the air is free from gas. The purity of the air can be tested by lifting the side of the facepiece of the respirator by inserting two fingers at the cheek and gently sniffing the unfiltered air; a fairly full breath should be taken in before the facepiece is lifted, and vigorously expelled after the test has been made, in order to blow any contaminated air from the respirator. If there is any doubt as to whether gas is present or not, the respirator should be kept on until this doubt can be removed. A rough guide to the smells of various gases is given in the Appendix "Table of War Gases"; they cannot be implicitly relied upon, however, since the presence of other constituents in existing known gases may alter their smell and so confuse detection. Any unusual smell should be regarded with suspicion, and where any doubt is felt it is recommended that the warden be consulted and asked for assistance.

Protection of the Body Against Blister Gases.

Protection of the body against blister gas, when this is present, may best be ensured by remaining under cover after a gas alarm has been sounded, until such time as the ringing of handbells by wardens pronounces the area "All Clear." There may, however, be cases in which contamination by misadventure may take place or be suspected, and it is necessary, therefore, to know the way in which the dangers might arise and the immediate steps necessary to overcome or to minimise the possible consequences.

The two principal blister gases are mustard gas and lewisite, and further information concerning them, including indications of the way in which their presence may be recognised, are given in the Appendix.

The respirator container will prevent the passage of the vapour of mustard gas and lewisite, and will thus protect the face, eyes, and respiratory system, but the remainder of the body will be liable to injury by exposure to the liquid or vapour. Ordinary clothing is of some value in that it delays penetration by vapour, or (to a less extent) liquid, and therefore the full effects of any contamination are not immediately produced on the skin. If such clothing is removed quickly and the skin thoroughly washed with warm water and soap, injury may be avoided, or very much reduced.

This procedure is intended to be followed by persons who are contaminated, or who suspect they have been contaminated, and are near their own homes or places of work, so that they can treat themselves promptly. Where, however, there might be delay, the outer clothing should be removed at once, and treatment sought at a public First-Aid Post. Here it will be possible for the person to wash, to put on clean garments, and to receive such first-aid treatment as his case may demand.

Persons who intend treating themselves in their own homes must remove their boots and outer clothing before entering the house, so as to avoid spreading the contamination and causing further casualties. Such discarded clothing and boots should be placed outside the house in a dustbin or other metal container with close-fitting lid, and steps taken at once for their removal and decontamination in accordance with local arrangements.

Decontamination of Contaminated Articles of Personal Apparel.

Ordinary Clothing.

Articles of ordinary clothing, such as overcoats, hats, coats, trousers, dresses, etc., which have been contaminated with vapour, should be hung in the open air for at least 24 hours. If the clothing still smells of the gas after 24 hours it should be placed outside the house in a container described above.

Light dresses and underclothing contaminated with vapour should be washed with soap and warm water, after preliminary airing, for at least 15 minutes.

Clothing which is, or is suspected of being, contaminated with liquid mustard gas should not be decontaminated at home, but should be placed outside the house in a container as already described.

Leather Boots and Shoes.

The decontamination of leather boots or shoes is a difficult problem, and all possible care should be taken to prevent their becoming seriously contaminated, by avoiding, for example, stepping into splashes or pools of liquid gas.

Persons who have walked through contaminated areas should in any case examine the soles and uppers of their boots to make sure that the boots are not contaminated with liquid mustard gas, taking care while doing so that they do not contaminate their hands. If any trace of mustard gas can be seen or smelt, the boots must be removed at once and taken as soon as possible to the appropriate place for treatment; meanwhile they should be left out of doors and not worn again until decontaminated.

Respirators.

Respirators which have been worn in blister-gas vapour should be thoroughly aired before being put away. If there is any sign of liquid contamination, the respirator must at once be returned to the appropriate quarter of the local authority, where another will be issued in its place.

CHAPTER 5.

SIMPLE FIRST AID
Introductory.

A complete organisation has been set up to deal with all types of injury caused by air raids, consisting of First Aid or Stretcher Parties, an Ambulance Service, First Aid Posts, and specially earmarked Hospitals.

Any injured person requiring treatment should go, if he is able, to the nearest First Aid Post. For those more seriously injured, First Aid Parties will render first aid and arrange where necessary for removal to a first-aid post or hospital.

There may, however, be occasions after heavy raiding when the services of first aid parties are not immediately available at all places where they are required. Often simple measures, if quickly taken, will save life; for example, in cases of extreme hæmorrhage (bleeding) or of true asphyxia (suffocation). Accordingly some of the elements of First Aid are described in the following pages, in order to enable those available at the scene of damage to assist the wounded while trained parties are on their way.

Wound Shock.

Every injury is followed by a condition known as Shock or Wound Shock, which is a failure of vitality varying in degree from transient faintness to extreme and dangerous prostration. In air raid cases Shock is likely to be very marked.

The condition can be divided into two stages, Primary Shock, which immediately follows the injury, and Secondary Shock, which may develop later as a result of excessive pain or bleeding or cold for a prolonged period or through clumsy or incorrect handling. Primary Shock may lead to Secondary Shock, if proper care is not taken, and this, if allowed to develop, may be dangerous to life.

Primary Shock can be treated, and Secondary Shock to a large extent prevented, by simple means :—

(i) Pain must be relieved ; for example, by gentle adjustment of the casualty's position, or by suitable support to the injured part before removal.

(ii) The patient must be protected from chill, since in cases of Shock body temperature falls rapidly. Unnecessary removal of clothing should be avoided, and the casualty should be wrapped in blankets or coats, with at least one layer between him and the ground.

(iii) Loss of blood must be checked.

(iv) Fractures or badly injured limbs or joints should be secured.

(v) Gentleness and smoothness are always essential in handling, lifting, and removing the patient.

(vi) Warm sweet drinks, such as sweetened tea, are of advantage to patients suffering from Shock, but it is dangerous to give any drink or food to an unconscious person, or to one who has a wound in the belly, or who complains or gives evidence of abdominal pain.

Hot water bottles are useful for protecting casualties from chill. They should be placed where they can best warm the circulating blood, for example, between the body and outspread arms, or the upper part of both thighs, since in each of these regions main arteries are relatively close to the surface and the warmth is circulated through the body by means of the blood stream. In doing this, care should be taken, by wrapping the hot water bottles in woollen or other material, to avoid burning the patient. They should never be laid directly on the bare skin.

Where a domestic hot water bottle is not available, an ordinary glass bottle, or similar container, wrapped in any piece of material or article of clothing, would make a suitable substitute. If an ordinary glass bottle is used, it should not be filled with boiling water, especially if the bottle is cold, as it may thus become cracked and subsequently break ; care should be taken in moving the casualty to prevent the bottle being broken and the casualty cut.

Bleeding (Hæmorrhage).

Profuse bleeding from a large artery immediately endangers life. Loss of blood is in any case one of the main causes of both Primary and Secondary Shock, and even the continued oozing of blood from an extensive area of the body may lead, if neglected, to collapse and finally to death.

Types of Hæmorrhage.

Hæmorrhage may be either external, in which case it is easily discovered, or it may be internal, caused by injury to blood vessels inside the body, from which the blood escapes into internal organs or cavities of the chest or abdomen. In the latter case, no blood is visible externally, unless it is coughed up or vomited.

Symptoms of Hæmorrhage.

The signs and symptoms of severe uncontrolled bleeding, either external or internal, are as follows :—

   (i) There is rapid loss of strength, accompanied by giddiness and faintness, especially if the patient is raised to a sitting or standing position.

  (ii) The face and lips become pallid, and the skin cold and clammy.

 (iii) Breathing becomes hurried and laboured, and may be accompanied by yawning and sighing.

  (iv) The pulse quickly becomes so weak and rapid as not to be felt at the wrist.

   (v) The patient becomes thirsty.

  (vi) He may become restless and throw his arms about or tug at clothing round the neck ("air hunger"), unlike a patient suffering from Shock without serious bleeding, who will lie very still.

 (vii) Finally, the patient may become wholly unconscious.

If these signs are observed, but no external cause is apparent, the case should be regarded as one of severe internal hæmorrhage.

Treatment of External Hæmorrhage

Blood escapes with less force if the patient is sitting and still less if he is lying, and the position of a casualty with external hæmorrhage should be adjusted accordingly. Except in the case of a fractured limb, the bleeding part should, where possible, be raised, to lessen the flow of blood to it. Firm, even bandaging with a pad of cotton wool or other soft material placed over the wound will normally help to check the bleeding.

In the case of a severely lacerated limb, bleeding should be dealt with by bandaging over a splint even though no fracture has been definitely recognised.

Treatment of Internal Hæmorrhage.

Internal hæmorrhage can only be treated on the operating table. The first aid urgently needed is warmth, extremely gentle handling and lifting, and rapid but smooth removal for surgical attention. Where there is even a suspicion of internal hæmorrhage, the patient should on no account be allowed to eat or drink.

Wounds in the Abdomen.

Casualties with wounds in the abdomen are more comfortable and less liable to further damage in moving if they are placed on the back, with the abdominal wall relaxed by bending the knees over a box, haversack, or rolled coat, and with the head and shoulders slightly raised. If any organs protrude, no attempt should be made to replace them, but they should be covered with lint, a soft towel, cotton wool, clean soft flannel, or similar material for protection, and the covering secured firmly, but not too tightly, with a broad bandage. It is desirable for the material used in contact with the wound to be wrung out of warm water to which, if it is readily available, table salt may be added in the proportion of one teaspoonful of table salt to a pint of clean hot water. On no account should a patient with an abdominal wound be given anything to drink.

Fractures.

Simple Fractures.

When bone is fractured (broken) and the surrounding flesh is undamaged, the injury is a simple fracture.

Compound Fractures.

When bone is broken and in addition there is a flesh wound at the site of the fracture, the fracture is said to be compound.

Complicated Fractures.

When bone is broken, and in addition there is damage to some important organ, the injury is a complicated fracture.

The following signs and symptoms may be present in cases of fracture :—

   (i) Pain at or near the point at which the bone is broken.

  (ii) Loss of power of movement in the affected limb.

 (iii) Swelling around the part affected.

 (iv) Deformity, the limb falling into an unnatural position and having an abnormal shape. It may be shortened by the over-lapping of the broken ends of the bone.

  (v) Irregularity : if the bone is close to the surface, a bump may be felt at the break and, if the fracture is compound, the bone may be exposed and visible.

Simple First Aid Treatment of Fractures.

(i) The first object is to prevent further damage being done by injudicious movement or by careless handling, and especially to avoid converting a simple fracture into a compound one, or causing an uncomplicated fracture to become complicated.

(ii) Unless the circumstances are such that danger to life is threatened, or that there is danger of further injury being caused if the patient is not immediately removed, the fracture should be attended to where the patient lies. The injured limb should be secured by splints or in some other way, and then the patient may be carefully moved.

(iii) If there is severe bleeding which is immediately endangering life, this must be controlled first.

(iv) Warmth and air are required to guard against shock which will certainly accompany the fracture. Blankets or coats should be wrapped round the patient, care being taken not to disturb him unduly. Merely covering the patient is often not enough to prevent him from becoming chilled.

(v) The limb should be placed in as natural a position as possible with great care and without using force. In the case of a compound fracture with a protruding fragment of bone, no attempt must be made to replace it.

(vi) If there is no material for splinting, a fractured leg may be secured by careful bandaging to the opposite leg, or a fractured arm by bandaging to the trunk.

(vii) Splints, real or improvised, must be sufficiently firm, and long enough to keep the joints immediately above and below the fracture at rest. The bandages must be firm, but not so tight as to interfere with the circulation of the blood.

(viii) Splints should be put on over the clothing and should, if practicable, be padded in places where there is risk of rubbing, or where there would be gaps between the splint and the body. Any suitable material which is available, such as clothing, handkerchiefs, or newspaper may be used as padding.

Improvised Splints.

Serviceable splints may be improvised from such things as laths from a venetian blind, from rifles, walking sticks, pieces of wood or cardboard, rolled up linoleum or newspaper, and a number of other articles, provided that the resulting improvisation gives sufficiently rigid support for the limb, and is long enough to prevent movement of the joints immediately above and below the fracture.

Improvised Bandages for Securing Splints.

Where the proper bandages, such as a triangular bandage, cannot be obtained, scarves, such as those worn by Boy Scouts, or pieces of cloth can be used. Ties, braces, straps, belts, or lengths of rubber tubing may be employed to secure splints or dressings.

Improvised Slings.

Slings may be improvised by pinning the sleeves of the coat to the garment, or by turning up the lower edge and pinning it to the main body of the coat. Improvisation may also be successfully effected by passing the hand inside the coat or waistcoat, which should then be buttoned. Scarves, ties, or belts loosely slung around the neck will also provide support.

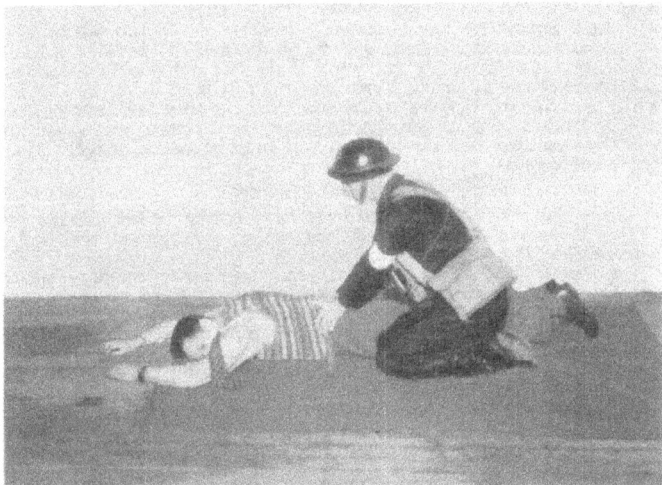

Artificial Respiration—Backward Swing.

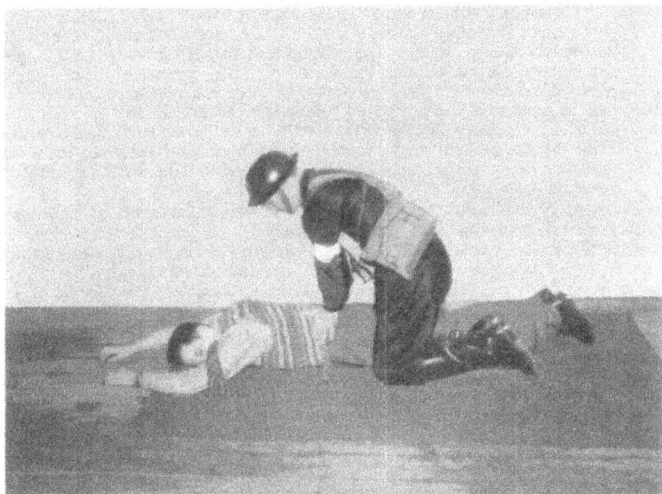

Artificial Respiration—Forward Swing.

55

Unconsciousness (Insensibility).

As a general rule, an insensible person should be laid on the back, wrapped in coats or blankets, with the head turned to one side ; if he has false teeth, they should be removed. If the face is flushed, the head and shoulders should be slightly raised ; if it is pale, they should be kept low. Any tight clothing, especially at the neck, chest, or waist should be loosened. Nothing must be given through the mouth to a person who is partly or wholly insensible. If an insensible person must be moved, smoothness and care are essential.

Suffocation (Asphyxia).

Anything which prevents the body from getting sufficient oxygen will cause a condition known as asphyxia, which, if unrelieved, will lead to insensibility and death.

Common causes of asphyxia under air raid conditions include electrocution ; continued pressure on the chest or obstruction of the upper breathing passages, for example, by debris ; confinement in a poisoned atmosphere (for instance, in an enclosed space containing domestic coal gas, exhaust fumes, or after-damp); and drowning.

The first action is to remove the cause of the asphyxia, or to move the casualty from the cause, whichever is the more suitable, and then immediately to begin artificial respiration, preferably by the Schäfer method, which is as follows :—

> The patient should be placed face down with his head turned to one side and his arms forward. The helper should kneel beside the patient facing towards the head and should place his hands on the small of the back, with wrists nearly touching, thumbs together, and fingers passing over the loins on either side. He should swing rhythmically backwards and forwards from the knees at the rate of about twelve double-swings per minute, keeping his arms straight, so that his weight presses the patient's abdomen against the ground and forces his abdominal organs against his diaphragm on the forward swing, pressure being entirely released on the backward swing. The pressure period should occupy two seconds and the period of relaxation three seconds ; to ensure regularity the rescuer should count evenly up to five on each double swing. This should be continued until natural breathing returns, when the rhythmic swing of the helper should coincide with the patient's respiratory movements.

Artificial respiration may have to be continued for an hour or longer, relays of helpers being employed if necessary.

While artificial respiration is being performed, other helpers should undo all tight clothing and wrap coats or blankets round the casualty.

Removal from Electrical Contact.

In cases of injury due to an electric current, the current should, if possible, be switched off at once. If this is not possible, it is necessary that the helper should himself be protected from becoming electrocuted, and for this reason he must place non-conducting materials between himself and the casualty, and between himself and an earth. Non-conducting materials, which may be available include rubber, linoleum, wood, glass, clothing, or newspaper. They should all be dry.

The injured person may be dragged away from the electric medium with a hooked walking stick or a loop of dry rope ; an umbrella should not be used since the metal parts will conduct electricity. Metal and moisture are good conductors of electricity, and therefore the helper should avoid touching the hands, armpits, wet clothing, nailed boots, or metal equipment of the injured person.

Burns (other than from Gas) and Scalds.

A burn is caused by dry heat, for example by a flame, hot metal, or a strong acid or alkali. A scald is caused by wet heat, for example by steam, boiling water, or boiling oil.

General rules for the treatment of all burns or scalds are :—

(a) Air should be excluded from the affected part as soon as possible. It should either be immersed in water, preferably at body temperature, or covered with clean cotton wool, lint, or soft clean cloths, and then bandaged. These are only temporary measures to meet the situation until suitable first aid dressings are prepared.

(b) If clothing has to be removed great care should be used. If it sticks, it is necessary to cut around the pieces of cloth which adhere to the flesh so as to leave them in position when the garment is removed. If blisters have formed, they must not be broken or punctured, but should as far as possible be protected and kept intact.

(c) Suitable first aid dressings may be made from strips of lint or linen about 2 inches wide ; they should be :—

either (i) soaked in warm strong tea and allowed to dry ;

or (ii) soaked in a lotion made by stirring baking soda in clean warm water. In this case the strips must be kept wet by repeated damping with the lotion which can be poured on over the bandage without necessitating its removal each time. The strength of the lotion should be about 2 teaspoonfuls of soda to a pint of water ;

or (iii) smeared with tannic acid jelly on the surface to be applied to the skin.

The dressings, which should slightly overlap, should be covered with cotton wool or soft cloth and lightly bandaged, and the affected part supported.

In severe or extensive burns, Shock will be marked and will require attention. The patient must be kept warm.

Gas Casualties.

Blister Gas.

If the eyes have been exposed to vapour or liquid gas, they should immediately be thoroughly washed with warm water or with a weak solution of salt or bicarbonate of soda; the strength in each case should be about one teaspoonful to a pint of water. If apparatus for eye-douching cannot be readily obtained, one of the following improvised procedures should be followed:—

(i) The casualty should bend over a bowl containing warm water or one of the mild fluids referred to above, and put the eyes, each in turn, well under water. They should be opened under water and the head moved from side to side.

(ii) The eyes should be opened in turn under a gentle stream of water from a tap, or from a rubber or other tube attached to a tap or hot water bottle, the head being moved slightly from side to side, and each eye opened and closed from time to time. Care should be taken to avoid contaminating an unaffected eye.

Any part of the skin contaminated with liquid blister gas should be dealt with at once. Where special anti-gas ointment is available, this should be instantly applied in accordance with the directions. In the majority of cases, however, this ointment will only be found at First Aid Posts and Cleansing

Stations and in the first aid equipment of Wardens and Casualty Service workers. An alternative method of treatment is therefore suggested employing solvents which are more usually in the possession of the ordinary citizen.

Liquid contamination may be removed from the skin by solvents such as petrol, spirit, or naphtha, and, since early treatment is vital, any of these should be used if it is more quickly available than ointment. To apply the solvent, a small piece of cotton wool or rag should be twisted into a pad and held between the finger and thumb, only the end being immersed in the solvent; as a further precaution against contaminating the fingers, a pair of oilskin or rubber gloves should be worn if they are available. It is important to avoid spreading the contamination by rubbing or by using an excess of solvent. The solvent only removes the blister gas by dissolving it; it does not destroy it. For this reason a succession of swabs should be used, and the contaminated swabs should be burnt or buried since they are dangerous.

Localised areas of contamination on the body should be treated as described, if the reagents required are readily available ; if not, the affected part should be thoroughly scrubbed with soap and water. In all cases where there has been contamination, it is advisable for the casualty to be washed completely with soap and water, in addition to the treatment described for the affected part.

In the case of exposure to vapour only, thorough washing with soap and warm water is sufficient.

It must be emphasised that the success of any method of preventive treatment depends upon the speed with which it is applied.

Lung Irritant Gas.

Whether symptoms are present or not, any person who has been exposed to a lung irritant gas must, from the outset, be spared any further exertion. He must be kept lying down and be protected from chill. He should be removed as a stretcher case.

Nose Irritant Gas.

The appearance of symptoms from exposure to nose irritant gases is slightly delayed, with the result that they may be felt a few minutes after the respirator has been adjusted. Any temptation to discard the respirator while still exposed to gas must be resisted. If vomiting occurs, the facepiece must not be removed ; affected persons should bend forward, turning the head to one side, and slightly raise the corner of the face-piece at the angle of the jaw while actual vomiting is taking place, dropping it into place between expulsive spasms. It is important that the facepiece should be allowed to fall back into place immediately, before the involuntary intake of breath which follows.

Summary

Where there are casualties requiring treatment and the Casualty Services are not immediately available, those on the spot, even if they do not know the precise treatment required, will very often be able, with elementary knowledge, to relieve the sufferings and possibly even to save the lives of the wounded.

The first consideration must always be to deal with any immediate danger to life. Examples of such dangers are excessive bleeding, interference with normal breathing (through pressure on the chest, obstruction of the air passages by debris or by electrocution), or nearness to moving machinery, tottering buildings, a spreading fire, or a poisoned atmosphere. In all such cases the source of danger must be removed from the casualty or the casualty moved away from the source of danger. After immediate danger to life, the second consideration is to try to avert or minimise injury, and the third to reduce pain and shock and make the casualty as comfortable as possible.

It may be convenient to sum up briefly some of the main guiding principles in elementary first aid :—

(i) Severe bleeding should be attended to at the earliest possible moment. This does not mean that every cut or wound should have prior attention. Discrimination should be used : the rule applies to profuse bleeding, the continuance of which would endanger life.

(ii) The casualty must be able to breathe normally : any cause of difficult breathing must be dealt with ; and artificial respiration, if needed, must be started promptly and maintained.

(iii) In cases of gross injury to a limb, whether or not a fracture is recognised, and in all cases of injury involving joints, the affected part should be supported and secured by simple methods before the casualty is moved, unless for any reason his life is in danger.

(iv) Any person who is, or has been, entrapped or buried under debris must be treated on the assumption that the severest crush injuries have been received. These might include fracture of the thigh, pelvis, or spine.

(v) A person who is wholly or partly unconscious, or one who is even suspected of suffering from internal injury, must not be given anything to eat or drink.

(vi) The indiscriminate use of alcohol in first aid can be dangerous ; it should not be given to persons suffering from any type of injury except on the direct order of a doctor.

(vii) All injured persons will be suffering from Primary Shock ; Secondary Shock, coming on some time after injury, may be fatal. Secondary Shock can, to a large extent, be prevented by the simple measures mentioned in this chapter ; it may be brought on or made worse by rough handling and clumsy movement.

(viii) Chill should always be prevented; and the casualty should at all times be handled and moved with the greatest care and gentleness.

NOTES ON IMPROVISED SPLINTS

When the proper splints are not available, it will often be possible to improvise suitable substitutes in a number of different ways, which will at least serve temporarily while trained persons with proper equipment are on their way. A few examples showing how articles in common use may be made to serve as improvised splints are given in the illustrations which follow.

If sufficient bandages are not available to correspond with the illustration, it should be remembered that the important points are to bandage above and below the fracture, and to ensure that the limb is kept rigid.

Sketch I.—Simple fracture through middle third of right femur (thigh-bone).

A broom used as a thigh splint by placing the handle along the injured limb, with the head of the broom at the feet. Loosely folded pieces of newspaper or other material may be used as padding, placed between the ankle and knee joints, and also at the hip.

Folded triangular bandages are shown in the illustration, but the improvised splint may be secured by any other material of sufficient length, such as, for example, neck-ties, belts, or scarves.

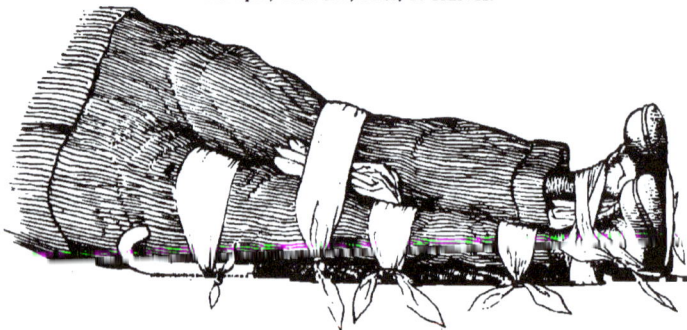

Sketch II.—Simple fracture through middle third of tibia (shin-bone).

The illustration shows an umbrella used as a splint. The ankles and knee joints are padded with loosely folded newspaper.

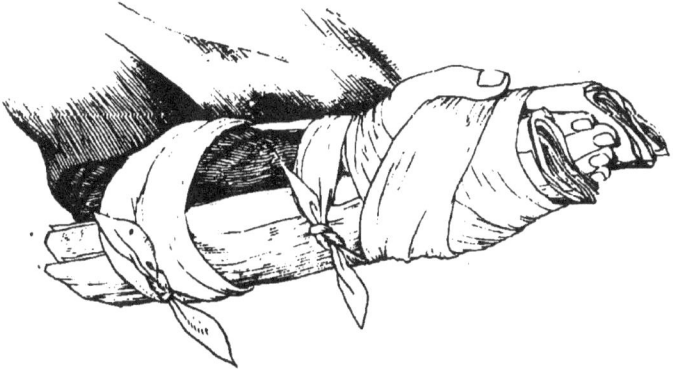

Sketch III. Simple fracture through one or both bones of the forearm.

The illustration shows the use of newspaper, folded to the approximate size of an arm splint, so as to be stiff enough to give rigid support.

APPENDIX

TABLE OF WAR GASES.

	1. Properties.	2. Odour.	3. Effects Upon Human Body.	4. General Function of Group of Cases.
Tear Gases. C.A.P. (*Non-persistent.*)	Solid; used in particulate cloud, almost invisible.	Aromatic, like floor polish.	Stinging of eyes, producing tears and spasms of eyelids. Slight skin irritation.	Mainly harassing agents producing temporary results; effective in very low concentrations.
B.B.C. ... (*Very persistent.*)	Yellowish-brown crystalline solid when pure, but probably used in brown liquid mixture. Invisible in gaseous state.	Penetrating bitter sweet smell.	Stinging of eyes, producing tears and spasms of eyelids. No skin irritation.	
Nose Irritant Gases. D.A. ... ... D.M. ... ... D.C. ... ... (*Non-persistent.*)	Crystalline solid of arsenical nature; D.A. and D.C. are colourless; D.M. is bright yellow when pure and greenish-brown when impure. When heated all give off a particulate cloud, which is generally invisible except near the point of release.	Practically odourless.	Burning sensation in nose, mouth, throat, and chest slightly delayed, accompanied by sneezing and mental depression.	Harassing agents with temporary results; effects felt after slight delay.
Lung Irritant Gases. Chlorine (*Non-persistent.*)	A greenish gas. It is a powerful oxydising agent, corroding metals swiftly and, more	Penetrating, like bleaching powder.	Coughing and watering of eyes; lung damage developing later.	

Agent	Physical properties	Smell	Physiological effects	
Phosgene (*Non-persistent.*)	slowly, rotting clothing, especially in the presence of moisture. Almost invisible gas. Corrodes metal.	Like musty hay, producing suffocating sensation.	Ditto.	Lethal agents.
Chloro-picrin (*Semi-persistent.*)	Colourless liquid, perhaps yellowish in use.	Similar to Chlorine.	Ditto. Has pronounced lachrymatory properties and produces vomiting.	
Blister Gases. Mustard (*Persistent.*)	An oily liquid heavier than water, varying from dark brown to straw-yellow. May produce iridescent stain. Emits invisible gas. Liquid and gas have great powers of penetration.	Similar to garlic, onions, horse-radish or mustard. May be faint or pronounced.	Irritation producing inflammation in eyes and throat, possibly resulting in blindness and lung damage. Reddening and blistering of skin. Symptoms delayed, appearing from 2-8 hours or more after exposure.	Highly destructive to all living tissues.
Lewisite (*Persistent.*)	Colourless liquid when pure, but brown in crude state; heavier than water. Emits invisible gas. Liquid and gas have great powers of penetration. Contains arsenic.	Strong smell of geraniums.	Severe irritation to nose and damage to eyes and lungs, possibly with permanent effects. Reddening and blistering of skin. Effects noticed immediately.	
Other Gases. Arseniuretted hydrogen (*Non-persistent.*)	Invisible gas.	Practically odourless.	Headache, nausea, and vomiting, with pain in the back and stomach. Severe symptoms do not usually develop till an hour or two after exposure.	Affects the blood, the liver and the kidneys.

SELECTION OF
OFFICIAL PUBLICATIONS

The series of Air Raid Precautions Handbooks and Memoranda has been produced by the Ministry of Home Security with the assistance of the Government Departments and other bodies concerned.

The Handbooks are designed to describe a scheme of precautions which it is hoped will prove effective in preventing avoidable injury and loss of life, or widespread dislocation of national activities. They aim at giving the best available information on methods of passive defence against air attack, and will be revised from time to time in the light of future developments.

The Memoranda deal with various aspects of the organisation to be provided by local authorities for public air raid precautions services.

HANDBOOKS.

No. 1. " Personal Protection Against Gas " (*2nd Edition*). **6d.** (8d.)

Gives rules of personal protection, and general knowledge of the nature and dangers of war gases.

No. 2. " First Aid and Nursing for Gas Casualties " (*3rd Edition*). **4d.** (5d.)

Provides information of both a general and technical nature required by nurses, first-aid parties, and the personnel of first-aid posts, to enable them to carry out their respective duties. Complementary to Handbook No. 1.

No. 4. " Decontamination of Materials " (*1st Edition*). **6d.** (8d.)

Explains the general principles governing the methods of counter-acting contamination arising from war gases. A text-book for the training of the members of decontamination services.

No. 4A. " Decontamination of Clothing, including Oilskin Anti-Gas Clothing, and Equipment from Blister Gases " (*1st Edition*). **3d.** (4d.)

This Handbook may be regarded as supplementary to Handbook No. 4, in which it will eventually be incorporated. For this reason, the Handbook is provisional only.

No. 8. " The Duties of Air Raid Wardens " (*2nd Edition*). **2d.** (3d.)

Gives an outline of the duties of air-raid wardens, and of the organisation under which they work.

No. 9. " Incendiary Bombs and Fire Precautions " (*1st Edition*). **6d.** (8d.)

This handbook, though written primarily for instructors, is designed also to serve as a general textbook on methods of dealing with incendiary bombs and the resultant fires. Demonstrates how the danger from incendiary bombs can be minimised, and why this can only be achieved with the co-operation of the general public and industry.

No. 10. " Training and Work of First Aid Parties " (*1st Edition*). **6d.** (8d.)

Concerns the organisation, training and work of First Aid Parties.

No. 12. " Air Raid Precautions for Animals " (*1st Edition*). **3d.** (4d.)

Intended for the guidance of persons engaged in the care and management of animals.

MEMORANDA.

No. 1. " Organisation of Air Raid Casualties Service " (*2nd Edition*). 6d, (8d.)

No. 2. " Rescue Parties and Clearance of Debris " (*3rd Edition*). 2d. (3d.)

No. 3. " Organisation of Decontamination Services " (*2nd Edition*). 2d. (3d.)

No. 4. " Organisation of Air Raid Wardens' Service " (*2nd Edition*). 2d. (3d.)

No. 6. " Local Communications and Reporting of Air Raid Damage" (*2nd Edition*). 6d. (8d.)

No. 7. " Personnel Requirements for Air Raid General and Fire Precautions Services and the Police Service " (*1st Edition*). 2d. (3d.)

No. 11. " Gas Detection and Identification Service " (*1st Edition*). 3d. (4d.)

No. 12. " Protection of Windows in Industrial and Commercial Buildings " (*1st Edition*). 4d. (6d.)

No. 13. " Care and Repair of Respirators " (*1st Edition*). 2d. (3d.)

Prices are net

Copies may be obtained at the addresses given on page iv *of the cover, or through any bookseller. Prices in brackets include postage.*

Wt 950.   6/40.   500M   S.E.Co.   51/7188   S.O. Code No. 34-9999

www.ingramcontent.com/pod-product-compliance
Lightning Source LLC
LaVergne TN
LVHW051802080426

835511LV00018B/3388